M000223605

A CIP catalogue of this book is available from the National Library of Australia.

Messenger, Lisa
Life & Love: creating the dream
ISBN 978-0-646-91359-9

First published in 2015 by The Messenger Group Pty Ltd
PO Box H241
Australia Square NSW 1215

Editing: Amy Molloy and Mel Carswell
Proofreader: Jen Taylor
Book design: Edith Swan
Photography of Lisa and Jack: Scott Ehler
Styling of Lisa: Lydia Saunders
Styling Assistant: Gemma Le Vin
Hair and make-up: Lei Tai
Clothing courtesy of: Aje (pages 30, 37, 62, 144, 148), Guess (pages 30, 37), Denisse M Vera (pages 16, 129), Lobelia Couture (pages 82, 90, 91, 100, 105, 108, 109, 112, 116, 120, 121, 160, 164), Ted Baker (pages 82, 90, 91, 100, 105, 108, 109), Lack of Color (pages 100, 108, 108, 109), One Teaspoon (pages 112, 116, 120, 121), Oskar (pages 160, 162, 164), Samantha Wills (pages 30, 37, 62, 82, 90, 91, 100, 105, 108, 109, 112, 116, 120, 121, 126, 129, 144, 148, 160, 164)

Instagram images on page 200 courtesy of @annahecek, @ashleaskye_, @blushingconfetti, @bonniecee, @frankiephotographyau, @i_heart_flowers, @jeskaalee, @lumedecor, @mcastelgrande, @ofkin, @rachelkareta, @rawstreetcreative, @redkittycreative, @scottehler, @sechysdary, @seewantshop, @shiraleecoleman, @starrey_em, @stylelifehome, @substanceblog, @torbdor, @twolittlepigsdownunder

This is proudly a Collective product
collectivehub.com

life & love

creating the dream

To my best friend,
soul mate
and love of my
life, Jack Delosa.

You are my
missing part.

You are my
everything.

To my Mum & Dad
for believing in
me and loving
me through
the whole crazy
journey.

I love you both
from the depths of
my soul ♥

Contents

INTRODUCTION

I am unapologetically, deliriously happy. I'm sorry if that admission makes you feel uncomfortable. I know it's far more socially acceptable to bitch about your life and focus on everything wrong it in, but I have to be honest and say I am happy. Pretty much every day. Really!

I know better than anyone how rare that is. You might look at me now and think that I have it all. I'm running a magazine sold in more than 35 countries, travelling the world public speaking and I'm gloriously (okay, sickeningly) in love with my partner. But it has taken me a looooong time to get here. It took a hell of a lot of pain, personal development and a long journey to become the 'me' you see before you (or are reading about) today, and that's what this book is all about.

I didn't intend to sit down and write such a personal book. After my last book *Daring & Disruptive*, which focuses on my entrepreneurial evolution, I had every intention of making my next book a how-to guide to building a business; the ins and outs, the dos and don'ts. But then this disruptor got distracted...

Like many of my light bulb moments, it came about when I least expected it – at 10.24pm on a Friday to be exact, when I was meant to be winding down for bed. I'd just had one of the most beautiful afternoons of my life. It was late September and after a long winter (by Aussie standards), the air was warmer than it had been for months and my partner Jack and I decided to play truant from our respective offices, sneaking off to a sandy cove near our house for the first ocean swim of the season.

I felt overwhelmed with gratitude – for the sun on my face, the salt in my hair and the man I loved more and more every day. After we came out of the ocean, I took a selfie of our smiling faces and posted it on my Instagram page. I decided

You can be soft and successful, a traditionalist and a rebel, a lover and a fighter, vulnerable and invincible.

decided not to care that people would know I wasn't at the office, that I'd taken the afternoon off (shock horror), and that our kissy-kissy couple's photograph was kind of soppy. I'm so grateful for this life, even if I have had to work hard to get it. A life where I can choose to take Friday afternoon off to refresh, rejuvenate and search out inspiration in nature, because is there any better place to brainstorm? At that moment I realised the book I really wanted to write was a book about love, joy, happiness, family, friends, community, laughter, purpose, authenticity, gratitude and all the things that mean so much when all the glitz and glam is washed away. I could write a guide on how to build successful businesses from the ground up. I could teach you how to balance a budget, plan a marketing strategy and harness some serious staff culture (and I probably will one day soon so watch this space). But the most valuable lessons I have learned don't fit within a standard business plan.

The real reason I am able to be daring and disruptive, to chase my dreams and search out profit in the seemingly impossible, is because I've spent years developing every pillar of my life – relationships, attitude, health and vitality – and exploring what it means to be a real human being in the business world. Wearing my heart on my sleeve, warts and all.

Let's be honest, I've f**ked up every area of my life at some point, but then I've rebuilt it to be better than ever. I've doubted myself... and then discovered confidence. I've been estranged from my family... and then learned no one is more valuable than your mother. I've had countless failed romances as I've struggled to juggle love and power... and then I allowed myself to be vulnerable and found love as a consequence.

Here's the truth: I spent years as a basket case, trying to discover who I really am via many (many) modes of personal development and spiritual camps in many pockets of the world. Now that I'm finally at the point where I'm comfortable with myself and I have nothing to prove anymore, I feel like it's my turn to pass the baton of knowledge, the map for self-exploration, on to you.

That's why I launched *The Collective* magazine in the first place, to build a community where we could inspire each other. My latest books – both *Daring & Disruptive* and *Life & Love*, which you will see are vastly different – are just another way to reach out to even more people at once. It can be a bit of a pain writing a book. It's a lot of time, energy and effort. Financially, I could invest my time in projects that are far more cost-effective. But as I always say, your core purpose shouldn't be all about profit.

While *Daring & Disruptive* was about identifying your business dream and finding your business purpose, this book is about putting the pillars in place – relationships, health and spirituality – to support your journey as an entrepreneur. It can be a relentless, exhausting road and you'll need self-love and support to sustain you.

Those of you who've read *Daring & Disruptive* might notice a difference in the tone and look of this book. This one is purposefully much softer, more feminine and more vulnerable. It's about family, friends, relationships, love, travel and embracing every side of yourself. It bids farewell to the '80s power-suited superwoman who could walk like a man and talk like a man (unless you happen to like shoulder pads, in which case, embrace that aspect).

I've been exploring the notion of masculine and feminine energy over the past few years. I am absolutely no expert and am figuring it out as I go, from observing, feeling and experiencing, but I think it's an important topic and I delve into it in this book because I spent so many years confused by the dual genders of my personality, the meek and the macho, the beauty and the beast.

I knew I was a strong, independent woman who could get (almost) whatever I wanted in the world, but at the same time I craved companionship and protection. I could kick arse in a boardroom with even the most intimidating corporate honcho, but I cried at romantic movies and when I came down with the flu, all I wanted was a caring partner to bring me chicken soup.

What I've learned is you can be soft and successful. You can be in love and ambitious. You can thrive on the adrenaline of business meetings but also enjoy having the car door opened for you.

You can be a traditionalist and a rebel, a lover and a fighter, vulnerable and invincible. In fact, that complex, confusing mixture of characteristics will only make you a better, more creative and likeable entrepreneur.

These pages are full of snippets and tidbits from my own personal journey, written from my heart, from one seeker to another. I truly believe we have a choice. We can choose happiness. And one thing I know for sure is that once you choose it and equip yourself with the tools to navigate to it, then the serendipity, synchronicity and the people, events and things you attract into your life as a result are beyond anything you could have ever imagined possible.

You don't need to be an entrepreneur or have any entrepreneurial intentions at all to benefit from this book. I wrote it for anyone with a yearning and anyone whose life feels a little off balance – we've all been there. Maybe you're a mum in the deep west who wants to experience more contentment, or a high-flying lawyer at a big corporation who wants to reconnect with her soul. Maybe you're already running a successful start-up and are constantly reassessing or tweaking your personal life to match the ride. I've learned there's never a full stop on self-development, there's always room for improvement.

I am not a guru and have never heralded myself as such. I am not qualified in much other than business. I'm just a country girl from Coolah, a town 495km from a big city. I didn't have anything handed to me on a silver spoon. I just chased after a dream and purposefully put myself in front of people who could enable me. I am an entrepreneur for entrepreneurs, but firstly I am a daughter, a partner and a friend. At the end of the day, I have a wealth of experience from the school of this thing we call life – and I'm more than happy to share it.

I want you to have it all, feel it all and experience it all too. This book is a beautiful indulgence about the things I have learned that have helped shape who I am, with the hope that it may help others navigate an increasingly competitive, crazy, fast-paced world full of pressures. I'm bursting at the seams to share my journey and inspire you to live your best life. Out loud. To be the best version of yourself. To be happy. Unapologetically.

My message is always this: anything is possible. Since launching *The Collective* just over two years ago, I have experienced things I never imagined in my wildest dreams. If this former basket case can have it all, then you can too. This is some of the journey. Thanks for travelling it with me, being bold and courageous and inspiring me every day. This is for you.

x Lisa

behind

the
scenes

I f you didn't know already, you will learn over the next few chapters that I am all about transparency. I am an open book (literally. You're on page 16 of it). So before we get into the nitty gritty topics of *Life & Love*, I wanted to give you a behind-the-scenes sneak peek at our cover shoot. Because, well, it was hilarious. You see that glossy, glowing, glamorous photograph of me on the front cover? I don't wake up every morning and climb out of bed looking like that. Being daring and disruptive, I seem to attract a certain kind of madness wherever I go, so transforming me into a cover star was, as always, a fun and crazy journey. Oh, where to begin?

As with my first book in this series, *Daring & Disruptive*, I did think twice about splashing my face across so many pages (me, me, me?) but I'm a visual person and the thought of a book full of black font on white paper really didn't excite me. Plus, although I'm not a prima donna, I wanted an excuse to dress up as a princess for the day, hang out with my friends in a park, frolic in the grass and generally muck around, all under the guise of work!

Unfortunately my choice of location – Sydney's Centennial Park because I love nature, fresh air and earthiness – isn't exactly convenient for a photo shoot. Think about it: no power plugs for the photographer's equipment, no mirrors for hair and make-up, a lot of people everywhere, a flock of geese who made a bee-line for me and a hundred outside factors that we couldn't control, from weather worries to bats pooing on my dress.

Yes, this happened. I was posing on a bridge, looked up, and a whole colony

car clothes rack

↑ Benny + his muddy paws

bulldog
clips

happy
snap

decided to bomb me. Not ideal when the designer dress in question is borrowed...

I should probably pretend that everything went smoothly to plan, a seamless, flawless operation. But I'm not about smoke and mirrors, and I'm happy for you to laugh at my mishaps. (Side note: to my wonderful crew, Scott my photographer, Lydia my stylist, Lei my make-up artist and their assistants, your staying power, resilience, capability and sense of humour are astounding and you could bring calmness to a cyclone.)

Let's just say I lived up to the title *Daring & Disruptive* when we descended on the park that Saturday. From my choice of 'changing room' (the side of the road, next to a 12-man cricket team and a bunch of their friends, who definitely got more than an eyeful) to my dog Benny coming over all fame-hungry and refusing to get out of any of the shots (after jumping into the muddy lake so he walked out looking like he had long black socks on – I'm so pleased I spent so long preening him to within an inch of his life beforehand).

What you can't see is that many of the dresses, which were too big for me, are held together at the back by rubber bands from our sushi lunch order and oversized bulldog clips. Also the horse you'll see later on. Well, it seemed like such a good idea to shoot myself resplendent on a horse – my first-ever job was as a horse riding instructor and I grew up in the country riding every day, so it was a poetic nod to my past. Unfortunately, the horse we borrowed was a little feisty. I was also wearing a giant tulle skirt, had a broken toe (that's a story for later) and had failed to mention I hadn't actually been on a (non-trail ride) horse for about 10 years. My favourite photo of the shoot is my crew cowering behind a nearby Mercedes Benz, which I was lucky I didn't land on and go through the windscreen, quite frankly, as I tried to cling to a "hangry" horse (apparently he missed lunch) that was bucking and running in circles. Said horse also had a role in *The Great Gatsby*. I bet it was better behaved for Baz Luhrmann.

But do you know what? Despite the chaos, despite indecently exposing myself to a sports team, getting pooped on by wildlife and remembering why you should

 the sushi band

behind the scenes

bulldog clips galore.

she designed a life she loved ♥

-Unknown

back at HQ

Bats!

crazy horse

designing away

I've had to learn to let people in, to be vulnerable, to ask for help.
—Lisa Messenger

never work with animals, I wouldn't change anything about this shoot. I wanted to be photographed on a backdrop that reflected who I am, and that's certainly what I got. I am fun, chaotic, spontaneous, unexpected, full of surprises and just a little bit wild sometimes. In business, people can become so confined by how they should behave, by how events should roll out. But there is no point writing an entire book about being the fullest, bravest, biggest version of yourself, and then having a photo shoot in a white-walled studio because it's 'safer'.

From my refusal to wear high heels (that damn broken toe), to my fabulous book editor Amy and her boyfriend arriving on their skateboards after getting utterly lost trying to follow my directions (I may be a little directionally challenged), the entire day was a true, authentic reflection of how I like to work and live – outside the box, against the grain, with lots of spontaneous fun that follows the road less travelled. It could have all gone horrendously wrong, but was somehow okay. More than okay. Wonderful. Hilarious. Unforgettable for so many reasons – but much more on that later. I always say that when things don't go to plan you have two choices – to freak out or to choose to look on the bright side, laugh at yourself and make the best of it. With every f**k up, I'd look at my editor and mouth her way "for the book", as she took notes on her iPhone, which at one point read, "bat poo, mad horse, boob flash".

During that entire day, even though I got changed 13 times, I never once looked in a mirror (we were in a park, I couldn't). But I didn't need to. I trusted my team completely and used their faces, their reactions and their emotions as my reflection. They all spent the entire day laughing – uncontrollably – and that was all I needed to see. So when you look at the pictures in this book (sorry if you get bored of my face) and are tempted to think that I'm perfect, that I spend my weekends wafting around beautifully in a forest, then just think outside the borders of the picture. There is probably a bat about to poop on my shoulder. But I will wipe it off, laugh it off and carry on smiling. You should too.

Now, let's talk *Life & Love*…

Our Deepest Fear

Our deepest fear is not that we are inadequate.
Our deepest fear is that we are powerful beyond measure.
It is our light, not our darkness, that frightens us.

We ask ourselves:
Who am I to be brilliant, gorgeous, talented, fabulous?
Actually, who are you not to be?
You are a child of God.

Your playing small does not serve the world.

There is nothing enlightened about shrinking so
that other people won't feel insecure around you.

We are all meant to shine, as children do.
We were born to make manifest the
glory of God that is within.

It is not just in some of us; it is in everyone.

And as we let our light shine, we unconsciously
give others permission to do the same.

As we are liberated from our own fear, our
presence automatically liberates others.

— Marianne
Williamson

attitude &

gratitude

Believe you can & you're halfway there.

- Theodore Roosevelt

I am a big believer in the universe sending you messages. Call it woo-woo, synchronicity, coincidence or just your mind playing tricks on you, but every now and again I'll see something, hear something or smell something that gives me a sharp reality check… just when I need it.

This morning I was training in the park before work. A few days a week I fit in a solid hour of boxing with my trainer, which I love. My dog Benny was running around in circles in the sunshine and I was having one of those epic exercise sessions where you feel fit, healthy, strong and the best version of yourself (as opposed to the ones where you feel like your legs are made of lead and you want to scream obscenities at your trainer).

In between upper cuts, I took a moment to take in my surroundings. It's amazing how often we walk around with blinkers on, not really 'seeing' what is around us. I'd been in that park for 20 minutes but hadn't noticed until then a group of young guys in hoodies, just meters away, who were drinking beer and, sadly, passing around a needle. At 8am on a Wednesday morning. As I tried to digest this scene, a garbage man strolled past me, stopping to pick up a chip packet on the grass.

When he saw me glance his way he smiled – a huge, genuine, open grin – and said with total sincerity, "What a beautiful day. How great is life!" He then continued on his way with a spring in his step, as if he was a tourist on holiday not a labourer at work. I don't judge the group of young guys who were self-medicating on that beautiful morning – that's their decision for life even though I am definitely not planning to make it mine. But the reason this reality check made me shiver was because I've had dark periods in my own life, where I was drinking to escape, drinking to forget and drinking to numb myself.

In my out of control days, that could have been me (although drugs were never my thing), I was lost and alone, living a life of guilt, fear, remorse and shame for a long time. It was interesting to stop and note the juxtapositions at play. Then there's this garbage man, with the most amazing, vibrant, optimistic energy, reminding everyone he meets how great life is.

The simplest messages at the most unexpected times can give us our greatest learnings. And I don't believe these reminders are accidental. As often happens with nudges from the universe, for me this one was perfectly timed. A couple of nights before, I'd begun to get the feeling that my ego was not in check and I was not the nicest version of myself. Okay, I'll call it – I had a braggy, self-absorbed, 'don't you know who I am?' moment. Ugh! I'm not proud of it, but I'm only human. It was quite a momentous time for me in many ways – I was about to celebrate my 10-year non-drinking anniversary and things were really, really taking off with *The Collective*. I could feel my mind racing away into 'it's not enough' territory. How could we change the world, the universe, infinity and beyond?

That's why I'm not surprised the universe decided to whack me over the head with a wake-up call this particular morning. It was time to stop and acknowledge my journey, where I was in that moment and the direction my life has taken, as opposed to where it could have gone. To take a moment to thank the universe and be grateful for the position I found myself in and for the lucky escapes, the near misses. And quite frankly, pull my head back in. So I said to my trainer, "I need to stop boxing." I needed to stop doing, stop fighting and to start feeling, enjoying and 'being'. I was in a beautiful park after all, so what better place to stop and smell the roses? That's why I called the first chapter of this book 'Attitude & Gratitude'. These two words sum up everything that I believe makes me a good entrepreneur, and even bigger than that, a good person to be around.

We are the directors of our own mindset.

We are all the directors of our own mindset. We may not be able to control outside factors, we can't stop bad things happening or ensure our path is pebble-free, but we can choose how we react to the annoying jabs, the pain and discomfort. *Daring & Disruptive* was all about identifying your 'why', finding your purpose and coming up with the big brainwave. In *Love & Life*, I want to give you the tools to put that plan into action and ensure that on the rollercoaster of life, you enjoy the ride rather than get motion sickness.

A lot of people – friends, colleagues and readers of the magazine – often say something like this when they meet me, "You're so calm. How do you do it?" The reality is I haven't always been like this, and like all of us, I still have my moments. I was once the fieriest person, prone to reacting quickly without thinking and flying off the handle. But as *The Collective* has taken off and life has become busier, even more overstretched and crazy, the calmer and more grounded I've become. Being stressed takes energy, arguments take time and these days, I am short of both.

I've trained myself to change my attitude to one of gratitude, even when I have seven meetings and three evening events to juggle in the course of one day, when all I want to do is go home and read a trashy novel in the bath. I could get in a grump and stomp my feet (and every so often I do) but that won't shorten the to-do list in front of me. So I have trained my mind to look for the positive in every situation. Hundreds of times every day, between getting out of bed and falling back into it, we can choose how we react, where we smile or frown, laugh or swear, give a compliment or a criticism that will raise someone up or knock them down.

MY FEEL-GOOD TOOL KIT

Endless optimism rarely comes naturally. Our culture likes to focus on the dark spot on the horizon. But over the years, I've learned a series of rituals and tools that help me to default to gratitude. These range from keeping a journal to a gratitude jar – when something good happens in your day, write it down on a scrap of paper and put it inside, then on bad days you can pull one out as a reminder of what you have to be thankful for.

I also have a little private ritual that I've never told anyone about until this moment. All day, every day, literally hundreds of times, I say a little prayer of thanks as I go about my business. Just two little words: 'thank you'. Sometimes I whisper them, sometimes I just imagine them. The traffic light turns green as I drive up to it: thank you. My green juice is the perfect temperature when I sip it: thank you. My partner Jack drops by the office: thank you. It takes less than a second and I do it so often it's become subconscious – an innate, ingrained ritual I do without noticing.

It's all about acknowledging the tiny, easily glossed-over events and moments that balance out the badness. It's like a flip that keeps me grounded in the positive. If I'm in the car sitting at an intersection and the driver next to me beeps for not moving fast enough, I've trained my brain to notice the beautiful tree on the sidewalk: thank you.

It doesn't stop the bad stuff happening to me. It doesn't stop me spilling my breakfast down my white shirt before a meeting or realising I've double-booked an important work trip on the same weekend as my friend's hens party. But it enables me to reassess my reaction. My brain is constantly switching, switching, switching, to move quickly through anything that's stressful.

I have other rituals I follow too. If I feel my emotions moving into a negative place – jealousy, envy, anger or insecurity – I imagine that my whole body is full of black, cloggy disgustingness like tar, filling me up from my toes to the top of my head. Then I visualise a tap releasing the thick, black liquid and watch it seep and ooze out of my body until I'm clean, light and bright again.

I love easy visualisation exercises like this because no one can tell you're doing them (a bit more subtle than squeezing a stress ball in a business meeting). Here's one for you to try: when someone really upsets you or drains your energy, imagine surrounding them in a pink bubble – once they are in a bubble they can no longer touch or effect you. I gently let that bubble float away. See the different energy here? It's all about letting them go, rather than screaming and ranting and raving. I have found this to be very, very powerful. Sometimes I'll take this one step further, and this might sound weird, but I have a beautiful little pink box that I keep in the freezer. Someone told me years ago that if someone is really upsetting you, write their name down and place it in a box (with love), put the lid firmly on and freeze it. I know, I know, it sounds woo-woo (trust me, as I write this I wonder a little about my sanity), however, it has helped me over the years.

These simple tools might or might not work for you, but they help me to move through emotional yuckiness. The best thing? These tools don't cost a thing, they take a matter of seconds to practise and what do you have to lose? You'll just have a little less space in your freezer!

THE POWER OF 'NO' AND PROTECTING YOUR ATTITUDE

On two occasions, I've actually walked out of business meetings before they were due to end. In both instances – and this takes some courage – the only explanation I've given has been, "I'm really sorry, but your energy doesn't feel right to me and I can't stay here any longer."

Yes, they've looked at me like I have five heads and perhaps I could have used less hippie language, but for some reason those words ground me and expressed how I felt in both moments. They reminded me to leave the toxicity, the negativity behind in the boardroom when I left and not carry it out with me.

It was about looking after me and honouring my boundaries, and in both of those moments I couldn't have cared less what those left behind thought of me. There is power in that.

It might sound wacky but I'm sure a lot of people reading this can identify. Whether it's a business meeting with someone who's drained you or a catch-up with an old girlfriend who just wants to bitch about people you both know. Perhaps it's a family member who is a glass-half-empty type and spends hours in a monologue about the slipping standard of society.

Another person's toxic energy can be draining, exhausting and demoralising and it's important to protect yourself. Make no apologies for doing so. As I've worked on myself and become more in tune with my core, I've also become more sensitive to other people's energy. That's why I now make a conscious decision to be around fun, uplifting, bright, light, positive people, because negativity is contagious and will hook you in. For me, this manifests by making me feel drained and worse, low and even sad.

Choose to be around positive, inspiring people and put yourself in places and spaces that uplift you. Most importantly, don't worry about removing yourself

LIFE & LOVE

from situations that aren't feeding and nurturing you. This rule still applies even if (and I'm sorry if I sound harsh here) the person in question has been in your life for a long time. I once had a mentor who said to think of life as a train – people get on your carriage, you may travel happily together for a while and then get off at different stations. It's not about judgement, but accepting you're on a different route. Everyone has their own journey, their own agenda, their own motivators, and sometimes other people cause you to be unnecessarily critical, negative and resentful.

There are so many people out there willing to point out your flaws – how your idea won't work, that you look too fat or too thin. The people in your life should give you momentum, pushing you forwards, and if they're not, then call an end to your journey or at least go your separate ways temporarily. Maybe your paths will cross again down the track. If it's meant to be, it will be.

This leads me onto the most import aspect of attitude for me – you are not your past, you can be anyone you want to be. Perhaps in the past you've been labelled a certain 'type' of person – a pessimist, an introvert, a troublemaker, someone who is ditzy, bright, quiet, difficult or conventional. It's not too late to change if you want to, to be whoever you wish to be, to break the mould and morph into any personality trait you wish to inherit. Nobody's personality or purpose is set in stone, and don't let anyone tell you who you are, or who you'll be forever.

If I'd listened to people, I'd still be working as a secretary in a real estate office, which is great for some people but it wasn't my passion and I had no genuine interest in it. It was my first real desk job after being a pony trekking instructor. I was there for 18 months and remember my dad saying when I quit, "Why would you leave such a great career path?"

Luckily I had the strength, stubbornness and thrill-seeking mentality to say that it wasn't for me. You have to allow yourself the courage to take risks, to be free, to hope for more and say 'fine' isn't enough. I think something fantastically fabulous is out there for us all.

Every day we have the opportunity to be reborn, if we give ourselves permission to forgive yesterday's mistakes – from the small to the big – and be liberated from the past. I wouldn't be the person I am now if I hadn't hit rock bottom around the lifestyle I was leading when I was partying, drinking and dancing on tables. Today I still dance on tables, only now I can remember it the next morning and I do it for fun, not because I need attention.

If you remain attached to those stories, those arguments, those 'ugh' moments that make you cringe when you think of them, you will get stuck. And what a waste of the rest of your life that will be. We all have the power to flip the switch, change our attitude to gratitude and illuminate not only our world, but everyone's around us.

Be gentle
with yourself
you're
doing
the best
you can

confi

dence

If I had a dollar for every person who's asked me, "Lisa, how are you so confident?" I'd be able to retire immediately. Not that I would. I'd go bonkers, can you imagine? But my point is, I've realised that confidence – or lack thereof – is an issue that people from all walks of life battle with. Forget the elixir of eternal youth, if a pharmacist could create a magic potion for confidence, it would be a sell out.

A lot of people don't understand how I can be so sure of my decisions, so relaxed around new people and stand on stage in front of a hundred suited, booted, bigwigs talking with so much self-assurance. But it hasn't always been this way. I wrote in *Daring & Disruptive* about how I overcame my absolute terror of public speaking via an extremely embarrassing gig where I totally froze on stage. We're all shy sometimes. Yes, everyone. Even that actress, singer, businessman, yoga teacher or politician who performs or stands before a crowd for a living. I read that singer Adele gets so nervous before going on stage that at an Amsterdam show she escaped out the theatre's fire exit, and she regularly throws up before her big moment. We all get nervous; we're only human.

But here's the important thing to ask yourself the next time your hands start to shake: what's the worst that can happen? Really? I have made a dick of myself so many times in life that when I had to think of a story for this chapter, it was impossible to just choose one.

There was the time I was hosting a big exhibition at Sydney's Convention and Exhibition Centre. I went to the bathroom (don't you just love a good toilet

story?). Well, I'm always fastidious about putting toilet paper all around the toilet seat when using public bathrooms (as my mother taught me) but on this occasion, as I hitched my skirt up and pulled down my pants, I realised I'd forgotten, so I twisted around to do it. I'm not sure, in hindsight, how I didn't notice the cubicle door had swung open, but everyone waiting in line for the toilets certainly did as one of the lead speakers at the conference mooned them. What can you do? I held my head up, took a bow and reframed it as a networking opportunity. At least I was memorable!

Then there was the time I took part in the CEO CookOff, a charity event where heads of businesses and famous chefs cook for people in need. In front of a large crowd of people I said to this guy in an apron, "So, what do you do?" and wondered why everyone burst out laughing. It was Bill Granger – only one of the best celebrity chefs going around. When I realised my mistake I could have dug a hole and buried myself, but instead I joked, "Well, do you know who I am?"

A friend told me she once went to a fashion show and said to a very prominent, very lovely female television presenter, "Oh I love your new hair cut. Pixie crops are very in right now." The group she was in fell silent and the presenter replied, "I didn't get it cut... I'm having chemo." Ground open up, NOW! But do you know what? If a mistake isn't made with malice, if you're trying to pay a compliment and it goes wrong, then there's nothing to be embarrassed about. My friend and the pixie cropper had a laugh and now have a fabulous relationship.

People get particularly nervous around so-called 'celebrities'. Hilariously, readers of *The Collective* say they're nervous when meeting me... me! I am in a funny industry where there's a real fame hierarchy, but I've never taken much notice of celebrities. Ask my team – they're constantly naming celebs and I'm saying, "Who's that?" It means I get laughed at a lot, BUT it also means I rarely get star struck, and I see people for who they are rather than the hype surrounding them.

When you meet someone who intimidates you, just remember that they will have felt intimidated by someone else at some point. Next time you're in a new

social situation here's a game to play: ask everyone about their biggest work stuff-ups. It's an awesome icebreaker and a total leveller, as I bet everyone, if they're honest, has a story to tell. The more experienced they are, the longer they've been in the industry, then the more extreme stories they've probably got to share.

I read that it is estimated one-third of the world's population would describe themselves as introverts, including performers such as Harrison Ford, David Letterman, Clint Eastwood, Meryl Streep, Steve Martin and Emma Watson. Think you're the only one? Then check out a Facebook group called 'Introverts are Awesome', which has over 92,000 followers. Sir Richard Branson, who I was fortunate enough to spend some time with recently, says he can't stand public speaking – in fact in his book *The Virgin Way*, he dedicates an entire section to the topic, entitled, 'I Loathe Making Speeches', followed by another section, 'The No-speech Speech'. It's well worth a read, as his philosophy on this is brilliant.

While I may appear totally extroverted, at ease and assertive, there are many occasions where I walk into a room on my own and quiver, "What am I doing here, who am I going to speak to, how long before I can get out of here?" It's not easy turning up at an event full of editors who've all been working in the industry forever, when you've just launched a magazine with absolutely no experience. You're an outsider and you know it. Remember at school when that new girl transferred from another city halfway through the term and everyone had already chosen their best friends? Yep, that was definitely me in mag land!

But the truth about confidence is you can fake it until you make it, it just takes practice, resilience and a few simple strategies to shift you from nervous to cool as a cucumber. I still have to draw on my reserves, tools and tactics that enable me to dig deep, take a breath and jump into a crowd of unknown faces. I always find it's never as bad as I expected. It's certainly more fun than wrapping myself in a cocoon, with only my own voice for company (blah, blah, blah!). The thing is though, most of those editors have been nothing but perfectly delightful and knowing the difficulties of running a magazine, have been in awe of our journey, very complimentary and extremely supportive.

You might be reading this thinking, "This doesn't apply to me. I don't run a business, I don't do public speaking, I've already met my soul mate and don't need to go out into the world promoting, parading and performing." But confidence isn't just about holding your own in big, brash situations. Everyone could do with a confidence boost sometimes.

I was recently asked to MC at one of my team's weddings. At the engagement party the groom (who was not used to public speaking) made what was possibly the shortest and most nervous speech, ever. He stood up, stuttered, "Thanks for being here", and then exited stage left before you could blink. He became the brunt of many a joke in the lead up to the wedding (aren't mates kind?) and so, with a few weeks to go, my darling friend asked me to coach him knowing that he would have to give another speech at the wedding. We went out to several dinners where I was meant to be coaxing him into it, but all he did was avoid the subject. I needed to think outside the box and find a new way to approach this! I needed to be daring and disruptive (hah, I could do this!). So I suggested that instead of making a standard speech, he and I could do a Q&A together on stage where I could lead him through his relationship journey. It would be fun, interactive and if he froze I could fill in awkward silences. Well, I needn't have worried about that because at the wedding reception, when I asked my first question he was off and running. I couldn't get another question in edgeways, which was fine with me. There wasn't a dry eye in the house as one of his stories flowed into the next. He went from being the brunt of his mates' jokes to the most revered speaker – and his new wife's hero!

This is the secret to finding confidence in difficult situations – always remember the hardest part is the first 60 seconds. If you can survive that – and still be standing – then the rest is easy in comparison. It could be as simple as having the confidence to turn up at your colleague's baby shower, even though you don't know anyone else. Or asking a waiter if they'd mind not putting the dressing on your salad. It could be finding the courage to sit at a shared table in a café, elbow to elbow with someone you've never met. Even if you think your friendship group, family and support system are already complete, widening your web of connections is always a good thing. Researchers from The University of British Columbia recently looked at the benefits of talking to strangers. Their study found that adults who engage with people they don't know with kindness also tend to be happier and less moody with their friends and family, compared to adults who just go about their business, blinkered and insulated.

If you want to find the secret to confidence, my number one piece of advice is to look your fears in the eye, say hello and shake a hand (even if yours is shaking). I promise it will get easier with practice. The more you can prove you can do it – and not shrivel up with shame and inadequacy – the more you will want to. Because guess what? Other people are really cool and can teach you a lot about yourself, including how confident you really can be.

love all.
Trust few.
Do wrong
to none.

-William Shakespeare,
All's Well That Ends Well.

LISTEN UP!

I recently spent the day at a water park with my partner Jack (we will always be big kids) and there was this long river ride where you sit in rubber rings floating along rapids. There were lifeguards along the sides and whenever we floated past one I'd call out, "What's the most memorable thing you've ever seen on duty?"

It may not surprise you to hear that of the 20 young, male lifeguards I asked, the majority of their anecdotes ended in "and then her boobs popped out". While their answers were pretty irrelevant, what amazed me was their enthusiasm and eagerness to share their memories.

Their faces lit up when I quizzed them, they literally jumped out of their chairs and jogged beside our rubber rings so they could finish their stories. It was such a simple moment with a series of strangers, but I like to think we all got a little higher, a little happier, a little smilier from this small interaction. It's a basic human instinct to want to be heard, 'seen' and acknowledged.

In the age of technology there are a lot of inhibitors that allow, enable and encourage us to be even more withdrawn and isolated – compounding a lack of confidence. We can order anything we need at the click of a button, we can bury our heads in our smartphones if we're feeling nervous and swap real friendships for social media relationships. I know that if I ever feel wobbly walking into a new environment, it often comes from a feeling of inadequacy. "Why will they want to talk to me? What can I contribute? What do I have to say that's interesting?"

Well, here's the magic flip in mindset. Having a conversation isn't just about talking, it's also about listening and, in fact, that second part is far more important. This is the mistake many people make – they feel pressure to perform, to hold the door, to be the funniest, smartest, wittiest, most entertaining person in the room, in the building, on the planet. Talk about pressure! But I've noticed that when I take a listening role in a conversation, ask questions and am really

The biggest key to confidence is acceptance. Of yourself & others.

When no one believed
in me, I did.

interested in what people are saying, I begin to feel genuinely involved, accepted and appreciated as a participant in that conversation. I now see it as a game – how many new people can I speak to today? They don't have to be long, drawn-out conversations. When I first got my dog Benny a few years ago, I was amazed at how strangers suddenly started talking to me as we walked along the beach. It was as if my furry prop gave people permission to reach out and connect (I imagine it's similar when you're pregnant or have a child). It made me realise how many people are eager to chat – if you give them an icebreaker. I love the awareness campaign by suicide prevention charity RU OK? They believe this simple question can build bridges and create community spirit, by encouraging us all to check in with each other regarding mental illness – without fear of isolation or judgement, no matter the answer.

It's not just our family, friends and workmates we can reach out to in every day life. Try it on the guy at the checkout, the stranger in the elevator, the neighbour you've only ever nodded to. How's your day? What have you got planned? I love your coat/shoes/handbag. Practise the art of proactive questioning. That means really listening to their answer, and then responding with real interest, encouragement and openness – rather than just waiting for them to finish so you can impart your next pearl of wisdom.

That's not to say you'll always get it right. I practise listening – purposefully – but everyone zones out sometimes. Years ago I was introduced to a prominent person whose surname began with "Moo…" That's the only bit I remember now… or could focus on then! A couple of month's later when I met him again, I couldn't remember his name. So I confessed, "I'm really trying to remember your name, but all I can think of are cows…" Luckily he laughed and the ice was broken. Confidence takes guts… and a sense of humour! It also takes practice and I still continue to test myself, putting myself in situations that push me outside my comfort zone. If I hadn't overcome my fear of public speaking, I'd never have agreed to attend the conference where I met my partner Jack.

1. Find a quiet couch

You don't always need to be at the centre of the crowd when attending a function or event. Sometimes I'll find a quiet couch to sit on in the corner on my own. Nine times out of 10, someone will come over, sit down next to me and we'll have a real, genuine, connected, present conversation (who wouldn't prefer a comfy chair to teetering about in heels?).

4 steps to events with ease

2. Set yourself a challenge

Set yourself a challenge not to look at your smartphone for half an hour. Look up, make eye contact, then smile! If you do want a technological crutch, try snapping some photos of the room, of the flowers, the view and the canapés. It's also a good conversation starter with other guests.

3. Give yourself permission

Give yourself permission to leave before midnight. I used to drink at events because it gave me more stamina, but now I allow myself to exit early, apart from scheduled occasions like weddings and award ceremonies. I network and have a good time, but I go home with a final, positive memory, rather than spending the last few hours watching the clock while engaging in small talk.

4. Take control

Take control of what you can. This might mean driving yourself to a party so that you have an escape route, researching the guest list in advance or bringing a plus-one with you. Taking ownership of an unknown situation is empowering and it will naturally boost your confidence and your contentment quota.

STRIP OFF, STAY TRUE

I recently posted a photo of myself wearing a bikini on Instagram. I'd never done that before and may never do it again, but I was at the beach, the water was beautiful and I was so happy that I wanted to share it. This is the reality of my day, this is the reality of my body (although I sure as hell sucked my gut in for the photo). I'm at that age where people around me start complaining, "Am I getting a bit too wrinkly, am I getting too old, what will people think of me?" I've been as insecure about my body as anyone in the past. It's tough not to be when we live in a culture of comparing, competing and judging, rather than facing our flaws with kindness, compassion – and even admiration.

One of the reasons I started *The Collective* was to snap out of this perfectionist mentality. I was sick of seeing airbrushed models in magazines when the reality is so different to the perception, which I'm realising more and more the longer I'm immersed in this industry. I'm not adverse to it either. Look at the photos for this book; I've had my hair done, my make-up applied, been dressed by a stylist and made sure the photographer shone a flattering light on me. I don't wake up like this! But in general, on all occasions, I try to present a true, honest, genuine, fully rounded representation of myself, even though it can feel easier to hide behind a mask of fake stories, exaggeration and empty compliments. Over the years, through much self-exploration and many uncomfortable social situations, I've learned that the biggest key to confidence is acceptance. This is me. I am here. What you see is what you get.

What's the worst that can happen? When you think about the scenarios that make your stomach twist in knots, what are you really fearful of? Tripping over as you walk through a room full of people? Accidentally offending the host? Having green stuff in your teeth or your dress tucked into your undies? I've done them all, and you know what? They're all pretty funny. The key to overcoming a lack of confidence is not taking yourself too seriously. The reality is that every time I try really hard to look cool, I fail miserably. It takes enough effort to get dressed up, trussed up and go out socialising at the end of a long workweek; I certainly don't have the energy to pretend to be someone else. And why would anyone want to?

If you think you're too old, too clumsy, too boring, too geeky, too loud, too quiet or too ordinary, then just think about all the people whose lives were cut short young, all the people missing from the family gathering, those whose names will never be on the party list, who were denied the privilege of this new experience. If I ever have a moment of self-doubt, I find this sobering thought snaps me back into reality. I can have the courage to say hello. Because it's sure as hell better than saying goodbye.

friends &

family

We find comfort among those who agree with us.

Growth
among those
who don't.

—Frank A. Clark

spent 10 years of my life largely isolating myself. I had alienated myself from my family; I was living under the same roof as a man but had never felt more alone. I had made the conscious decision to cut all ties with my mother – a decision I thought would empower me but only served as a domino effect to alienate myself from the rest of my family. Our struggles began when my parents divorced and over time the tension grew to toxic levels. I remember when I married my first husband – my ex-husband – instead of coming to my wedding, my mum and sister walked the Inca Trail. I can't blame them. A mountain goat would have been better company than me at that point.

But all was not lost! Fast-forward 11 years to the launch of *The Collective* in March 2013 and on the night of the launch party, my mum and my sister Kate came to my home and we all got dressed together. My whole office was filled with bouquets of flowers sent by well wishers, and I remember we were picking each other's outfits, reading the cards and eating our way through the boxes of chocolates I'd been gifted. It was a beautiful, girly, intimate celebration of the three of us long united. Best friends in the world. It was like the wedding they didn't attend.

That's why I want to honour my friends and family in this chapter, and be honest, open and transparent about our journey. I've since met so many people who say, "You're so lucky you have the most amazing relationship with your family", but it certainly hasn't always been that way. I've had to learn to let people in, to be vulnerable, to ask for help (and undergo an intensive cathartic program

What is done in love is done well.

-Vincent van Gogh

of The Hoffman Process, most of which involved hitting inanimate objects with a baseball bat) to get here.

But it was worth it. I learned that I didn't want to live as an island. For me, it was a far cry from paradise! I'm forever grateful I had the courage to ask for forgiveness, to say I love you without expectation, and that my beautiful family were so receptive and forgiving when I did. Sometimes it can feel easier to hate than love. We hope that anger will make us feel powerful, in control, dynamic and driven. But here's what I've learned – you can be a strong, independent woman (think Beyoncé) and have genuine, passionate, nurturing relationships.

Since my family reunited, I've learned that as amazing as my career is, no matter how much I thrive on *The Collective*, the hype and the spin, the real moments that refuel my soul, my energy and my spirits are those I share with my family. The walks on the beach, the cuddles with my niece, the year my mum and I flew my sister to Bali as a surprise for her birthday, sailing tugboats on the dam with my dad. Love really is the only currency that matters.

I've had to learn to let people in, to be vulnerable, to ask for help.

WHO IS YOUR MUSE?

I'll admit it – I used to be neeeedy (say it in a whiny, pleading voice). I can see now it started when I was just a little girl, struggling with my parents' divorce, trying to get the attention of my mother and to boost my insecurities by pleasing, impressing and astounding her. Unfortunately I didn't grow out of it – until I was in my thirties anyway! – and it had a knock-on effect on my career path.

I wanted to make my businesses grow, be the biggest, the loudest, the shiniest, for no other reason but to show my mother I was 'winning'. The problem was, because my intention, my purpose, my 'why' wasn't pure and I was coming at my career from a place of ego, I still never felt good enough. I remember I would drag my poor mum to awards ceremonies where my business was being honoured, and we'd end up having a massive row because I didn't feel she was clapping *enthusiastically* enough. Even if she'd given me a standing ovation, with a brass band, fireworks and an "I love Lisa" banner it wouldn't have been enough. My ego was *that* fragile.

But when I launched *The Collective* it was a totally different story. My 'why' wasn't to impress my mother, and so she became my collaborator rather than my target. I remember sitting down and telling her that I wanted to launch a magazine that would shake up the industry, that it wasn't about me, but changing the world, building a movement and making a difference. I then asked her opinion, her advice and really valued her answers. This time I didn't want to succeed just to impress the woman who gave birth to me – I wanted to succeed to inspire hundreds, thousands, even millions of people.

Ironically, that shift in mindset actually brought us closer together. I'll never, ever forget the moment I was with my mum and we saw the first issue of the magazine in a newsagent for the first time. We were both screaming, laughing, crying and jumping, so loudly that the newsagent's owner came to check on us.

"Are you okay, is someone hurt?" We looked like mad women but it was such a beautiful moment to share; the two of us losing ourselves in beautiful, chaotic emotion. I'd love to see the CCTV video. Can you imagine? Forget posed family photos, these are the moments to remember. There have been so many beautiful, connected moments like this since and my family are my number one supporters. I am grateful beyond words for them every single day.

FIND YOUR TRIBE

A few years ago I bought a holiday house in Bangalow, near Byron Bay in New South Wales, Australia. The house had every colour on its walls when I bought it – nasty shades of chocolate, salon pink and a particularly pukey shade of tangerine. We needed a white out! So I invited a bunch of my best friends to the property for a long weekend to do a quick four-day renovation (bribing them with the promise of wine and free dinner). Here's the thing – I had never painted a house in my life, as was proven when I painted over a power point, and then in my enthusiasm to fix it, decided to dig said paint out of the socket with a metal screwdriver. I'll never forget my friend Luke's holler as he lunged to stop me electrocuting myself. Unfortunately, in his haste to save me, his long-handled paint roller had a collision with the overhead ceiling fan. Paint sprayed all over the kitchen, Luke nearly dislocated his arm, and we both ended up in a heap covered in white paint, as if we'd been at the wrong end of a flock of seagulls. For anyone under the impression that I'm remotely cool or classy, this incident should put your mind at ease. As for my best friends, they wouldn't expect anything less. They know I'm the biggest dag – and that's why they're my people.

True friends know you don't get it right all the time,

they see your
flaws & will
be there
when you fail.

I think 'popularity' is a funny word because in the age of social media, it's all about the numbers. How many followers do you have, how many friends on Facebook, how many people 'like' you? But for me, it's all about quality rather than quantity. How many real friends do I have in my life? There's a decent handful, that's it. But I'd take a bullet for them, they're my bosom buddies, I love them deeply and I know they feel the same about me.

Unfortunately it hasn't always been this way (do you see a pattern developing?). I've sometimes been a truly terrible friend, self-absorbed and focused on my own worth, with my head stuck up my arse (it's still there from time to time but I have a lot more awareness around it and the ability to pull it out). In my 'Loopy Lisa' drinking days, I often thought about investing in a florist because of the amount of 'I'm sorry' bouquets I had to send to friends the morning after the night before, when I'd had a loose-lips-sink-ships kind of night. Again. And again.

But they say the most memorable people in your life will be the friends who love you even when you aren't lovable. And thank goodness for these kind, forgiving, generous souls (you know who you are) because I've learned that everyone needs friends. Not hundreds. Not even a dozen. Life is busy and it takes time to nurture such genuine, deep, committed relationships. But enough friends to balance out the 'yes' people in your life, especially when you're running a business. I get bored of myself, bored of my stories that I've heard a hundred times and bored of the sound of my own voice. I need people to reign me in, offer constructive criticism and keep me anchored, grounded and 'just Lisa'.

LIFE & LOVE

the most memorable people in your life will be the friends & family

who love you even when you aren't lovable.

STOP NETWORKING,
START LOVING

I can separate my social life into two categories – the stuff I choose to do because of work and the stuff I choose to do because it feeds my soul (luckily they are often one and the same); the events with people I should meet and the events with people I'd climb mountains to hang out with. (Side note: this is why I'm careful who I invite to *The Collective*'s events. I love bringing together a roomful of strangers who are on the same wavelength and genuinely interested in connecting, but unfortunately some events I'm invited to are just full of "fakies" with big egos, who only want to shove their business card into your hand.)

I've been fortunate to go to some glitzy parties at some very glitzy places, but that's all just interior design and fancy furniture. The real pillars that matter are my people, who have the power to fill a bare room with no windows with their lightness, brightness, colour and laughter. Case in point – New Year's Eve a few years ago. I invited my friends Josh and Jules to my Bangalow house (with its new paint job) and heard about a cool party happening in the hinterland nearby. In my head, I imagined a Bohemian, barefooted, lantern-lit dance party, with a hippie kind of vibe where we could chill, chat and maybe play some bongos. The reality was a little different. When we arrived at the address it was a local community hall with bright fluorescent lights, kiddies running around and pensioners sipping on cups of chai. Not exactly the celebration I'd promised my besties who'd flown up from Sydney to spend time with me. It was hysterical – hysterically bad. But it's a night we still talk about; we bonded over the anti-climax, the absurdity and the fact that only I would put them in such a surreal situation…

Here's the thing about true friends – they know you don't get it right all the time, they see your flaws and don't blow smoke up your arse. Thank goodness. When you're an entrepreneur with ambitious goals and a can't-switch-off mentality, it can be easy to fall into the trap of seeing everyone you meet as a building block in your yellow brick road. You instantly assess new people; who do they know, what are their skillsets, how can they get me to where I want to go? But real friendships aren't about networking or using each other for professional gain. Very few of my closest friends are actually business people. Two of my best friends are church-going, surfy mates who I love because they make me laugh and we can be goofy together. They know little about running a start-up, but they are two of the most soulful, incredible, down-to-earth, loving people I know. The hats we wear in our day jobs are irrelevant. When we're together we talk, we share, we listen, we laugh and we connect on a far deeper level than just our jobs.

There is a big difference between friendship and idolisation and, as much as I value all of the emails, tweets and messages I get from strangers saying that I'm amazing (seriously, I have been known to cry at my desk in appreciation and wonder several times a week), I have to make sure it doesn't go to my head and keep it in perspective. I equally value the emails that I get from *The Collective* readers who (on rare occasions) say, "I feel like you let us down this issue Lisa" or "I think you should include more about this topic". I don't want to surround myself with 'yes' people who pump me up all the time because then how would I learn, develop, grow and become a fuller version of myself? I am not perfect and I need people in my life who remind me of that – and love me anyway.

Since I made a conscious decision to be more present, authentic, genuine and available to my friends, I have felt all of my important relationships drop to new levels, deepen and strengthen. Suddenly friends have started asking me to be their bridesmaids and play significant roles in their lives – even though they know I'm likely to be the one who falls on the wedding cake while trying to bust out a ridiculous dance move.

They know I'm not perfect, yet I'm still the one they know they can rely on, call on for help and lean on for guidance. As I started to work on myself and, most importantly, when I was able to rely on myself, others felt they could rely on me too. So seek out your true tribe, nurture them and make time for them.

The friends who tell you the truth even if their voice shakes, those who offer criticism with grace and will comfortably sit with you in silence. You can make millions of dollars of profit, win every business award and be fought over by investors, but nothing will match the glow of real, heartfelt connection with another human being.

love,
love,

love

The funniest thing happened when I sat down to write this chapter. The second I typed 'love' at the top of a new page, I kid you not, literally that exact second, I received a phone call. It was 10.30am on a Monday morning, I was sitting at my desk and my phone started ringing with my favourite name flashing up on the screen. A person whose voice still gives me butterflies every time I hear it. Jack. My soul mate. My best friend. My entire world. Was he calling to check up on me? No. He was calling because, once again, he'd managed to embroil himself in a crazy, hilarious set of circumstances. "Babe, I'm locked out again. I went outside and the wind blew the door shut. Can you send your keys home in a cab?" The most ridiculous part about this – it was the second time he'd done it in a week. The most hilarious part – he was only wearing his underpants (I'm still not sure exactly why he went into the front garden in his undies but perhaps that's for another day). I could have been annoyed at the inopportune interruption, but all I could think was, "This is why I love you, you crazy, little nutter."

The taxi driver was more than a little suspicious when my assistant handed over my house keys with my address and instructions to look for a half-naked man waiting in the front garden...

Love is a humongous topic to try and tackle. I'm no expert, not even close, but I have spent a fair amount of my time on this earth failing at it, and in equal measure trying to find a way to get it right. I have seen similar journeys to my own play out in the lives of people in the business world and, for that reason, I am willing to share some of the journey and the lessons and insights I've gleaned along the way. I am no Love Doctor, but I have previously suffered from love sickness – and I'd say I'm now in remission. So while I can't give you a magical

cure – for how to let yourself be vulnerable, for how to find the 'one', or when you do find them how to manage the infamous 'juggle' – I can share my own rocky experiences. And hopefully it will give you a starting point, or at least some motivation not to give up hope. Because if I can find true love, and maintain it despite a schedule that leaves me little time to go to the bathroom, then truly anybody can. Believe me!

Where did it start for me? My first kiss was at pony camp when I was about 13 sitting among a bunch of hay bales. There were about 12 of us and one of the boys announced that we were going to sneak away from the parents. We all knew the reason; we had a pact it would happen. Not exactly romantic – it was more contrived, awkward and embarrassing. I had a 'boyfriend' at the time – Ben – although until that point our relationship only consisted of a few phone calls from boarding school to boarding school, a bunch of love letters illustrated with big hand-drawn red hearts and some sweaty-palmed hand holding. I'll never forget, before our first kiss, the ringleader of our gang Doug gave us a series of instructions: don't put your tongue in, keep your eyes closed, decide beforehand which way your nose will go. All the important stuff! Then we all paired off and went to find a quiet corner. Was my first kiss seamless? Not exactly… As soon as our 'peck' was done I turned around and looked for the nearest exit, only to fall straight into a hole in the floor of the wool shed. And so my rocky relationship with love began.

I like to recall this story, because it reminds me how ephemeral a heart's desire can be. Back then having my first kiss seemed so, so important, and it was a milestone we talked about for months and months afterwards. While I was working on this chapter, a friend showed me a page from her diary as a 13-year-old, where she had drawn a detailed diagram of her first kiss – with their exact lip position – just in case she forgot how to do it. Now, when we're in a relationship, kissing is something we do (hopefully) day after day, week after week and there is a danger it becomes just like brushing your teeth – perfunctory, mundane and insignificant. Imagine if every kiss carried the same adrenaline rush as your first? Where our world feels like it's shifted so vastly that we feel like we've fallen through the floor (in my case, literally). I hope mine always will.

Where did your own romantic adventure begin? What did "true love" mean to you, before society, culture and Ryan Gosling in *The Notebook* conditioned what you thought it looked like? I find it interesting to analyse the moment your classmates – the ones who visit a different bathroom and wear trousers instead of a skirt as part of their school uniform – suddenly shift into objects of desire; when something in your mind clicks and they go from "icky" to "irresistible" overnight, transforming the way you act, communicate and see the opposite sex – forever.

I was sitting on the beach the other day watching two little kids play tag – a boy of about seven was chasing after a little girl, who was wearing a frilly cossie and sprinting through the shallows of the ocean. She looked so unabashed, so unselfconscious, so utterly free and liberated. It hit me that in maybe only a matter of years, this same little girl probably wouldn't run in front of that boy because she'd be too concerned her bum would wobble, or that she'd make a fool of herself. I hope I'm wrong, but I doubt it, and what a shame that is. Because I don't think I've ever seen an adult look as joyful as those two children that day.

In *Daring & Disruptive*, I talk in depth about the importance of approaching business as the fullest version of yourself. I truly believe the same should apply to romantic relationships. Yet, so many of us – myself included – are guilty of shrinking ourselves to attract a partner, so that we don't intimidate, overwhelm or appear "too much" in general. Instead, I urge you to be that little girl sprinting in the ocean with her little chubby bum bobbing. Growing up is overrated – in life and love!

YOU'RE WEIRD – I LIKE YOU

Our romantic mindset naturally shifts as we get older and we realise love isn't exactly like we see it in the movies. All of my teenage dalliances were pretty light-hearted; I rebounded quickly and the scars they left on my heart were minor. But as I moved into my twenties, things started to get a little more serious – and subsequently fell apart with lightning speed. The problem was I hadn't really connected with my true self yet, and in hindsight I can see I had abandonment issues that at the time I blamed on my parents' divorce (although they were probably of my own making). (Side note: now I've learned to reframe my parents' divorce as a positive. As Oprah Winfrey says, "The struggle of my life created empathy – I could relate to pain, being abandoned, having people not love me.")

Whatever the cause of my issues, I would perpetuate the same patterns over and over. I'd get into a new relationship and quickly become needy and clingy – don't leave me, don't leave me, PLEASE don't leave me! Of course when you do that, they all leave you! (Imagine me running down the road, wrapped in nothing but a bed sheet, which then got tangled around my legs and left me sprawled in a gutter. Bridget Jones eat your heart out!).

I never had a problem getting a boyfriend (I was young, funny and unpredictable) but keeping them was another matter. I was in a constant cycle of three-week relationships throughout my twenties and early thirties – aside from a brief stint as a wife, which was the loneliest period of my life (that wasn't his fault, he was a lovely, sweet, caring guy, but we just hadn't done the work to know who we were yet). In all my failed relationships, I was starting to see the common denominator: me. And that is not a comfortable realisation for anyone, let alone a perfectionist who has kidded herself into believing that "it's not me – it's them".

So I did what I do best – I decided to change. As you may have noticed by now, I am never satisfied with having a problem and not doing everything I can to personally solve it. I read books, I sought help and despite having very limited funds at the time, I scraped my spare cash together to attend courses as far reaching as a two-week stay in a raw food, vegan "love commune" in the Costa Rican jungle. I thought it sounded quite… sexy. A retreat in the middle of the jungle. (This was years before *Eat, Pray, Love* came out so I can't even blame that for my misconception.)

The reality was very different. When I arrived, it was pouring with rain and I was so freaked out by the old, hairy hippies inviting me back to their "casita" to make love to them that I burst into tears (I probably gave the poor guy a lifelong complex). But do you know what? I stayed the entire two weeks – in my own bed, without any strange company – and the weird and wacky situation made me assess who I was, what I wanted and how to move forward. Was I too much of a prude to run off into the jungle and have wild sex with this man? Yes. Okay, so what did I want? A real, genuine connection with someone, which would hopefully last a lifetime.

While we're on the subject of free love, that reminds me of another boyfriend, who shortly after we met told me he just wasn't into monogamy and wanted an open relationship. Gulp! I'm happy to report that I didn't indulge in threesomes. Despite this, it was one of the relationships (albeit short lived) I am most grateful for because it threw my rule book out the window.

When you grow up, it's easy to slip into the trap of living life according to other people's values, expectations and belief systems. But this particular boyfriend and I would have endless conversations into the night, talking about philosophy, psychology and whether human beings are made to mate for life. It gave me the opportunity to truly know who I was and what was important to me. I knew for sure then and there that monogamy was the path for me. But now it wasn't just because society had told me so, it was because I'd delved into my desires and reached my own conclusion.

It also stripped away my judgement and caused me to be far less critical. Mr Polygamy was actually a kind, decent guy. He just happened to view relationships from a different angle than I did. You could argue that at least he wasn't trying to hide or deceive and was acting from a place of honesty and authenticity.

Wouldn't the world be boring if we were all the same and had nobody to stretch or test us? On day one of the aforementioned "love commune" I met a guy called "Sparkle" who described himself as a "radical faerie" (it's a thing – Google it). My barriers came up, my judgement on high alert. But by the end of the week I was embarrassed at my initial feelings. He had stepped straight into who he was and was owning it 100 per cent, no apologies.

I love the quote from American author Thomas Meron who said, "Our job is to love others without stopping to inquire whether or not they are worthy. That is not our business and, in fact, it is nobody's business. What we are asked to do is to love, and this love itself will render both ourselves and our neighbours worthy." I am not saying you should pursue multiple lovers (who has the energy?) or run around with fairy wings on, waving a sparkling wand. But how many of us are trapped in a template of how love should look and what makes a perfect partner? What happens when you step out of the box and rip up the rule book?

LOVE AND LEADERSHIP

You might be reading this thinking, 'that all sounds like a lot of hard work!' Well, yes, it was. It's true that, in the pursuit of love, I really put in the legwork. This is a topic that I've debated into the night with my girlfriends: should you pursue a partner or let them arrive into your life in due course? In my experience, it's about reaching a happy medium. I am a woman of positive action, but not everything in life can be slotted into a business plan.

In many of my relationships, I'd never been in them for the right reasons. As well as my childhood issues with abandonment and coupled with fast boredom, as I became more successful in business, my behaviour in relationships became even more toxic because I wore my 'boss hat' home. I tried to micromanage, control and organise my love life as though my boyfriend was a staff member who needed constant instruction, encouragement or promotion. I have seen similar scenarios play out over and over again for many single women I know, now that I have finally figured it out for myself (I'm a slow learner!). That's part of the reason for devoting an entire chapter to this, because it seems to be a recurring issue among fearless, female leaders who have positions of power.

A very successful, very ambitious and very affluent girlfriend of mine recently started dating a guy. She showered him with gifts, invested in his business and flew him around the world because she was going to a conference in Europe and wanted him there with her. Then she wondered why he wasn't being attentive and didn't seem happy or excited to see her. I don't want to sound judgemental, I did variations of this for many years. I kept wondering what was wrong with me, as I was being so "helpful" to these men, encouraging, enabling and pushing them to greatness. Yet I was almost smothering them. I was the walking, talking cliché of the woman who always wants the bad boys (maybe I thought I could fix them?) and pushes away all the nice guys. I've always been into instant satisfaction and had a penchant for fast-tracking everything.

So the question is: what changed? Because as I revealed at the start of this chapter, I now have a wonderful man at home (or standing in the garden in his underpants). A man who doesn't need me, but wants me, a man I don't need to "fix" but who asks for my input because he genuinely values my opinion. I don't like to make out I had one great epiphany, because my romantic history is full of lessons, transformation and development. However, I know that many of you will be looking for guidance so I will reveal one game-changing moment. Or, one game-changing person to be exact – Rori Raye.

When my beautiful sister recommended a must-read book: *Have the Relationship You Want* by Rori Raye, I didn't realise how significant this purchase would be for me. Isn't it amazing how such a small decision – to go online and add a book to my basket – can change absolutely everything? I know, I know, it sounds like a book a desperate heroine would read in a rom-com; the type of book you'd be embarrassed to read on a plane or a train, and I was sceptical at first too. But I found myself transfixed by this step-by-step women's guide to transforming your love life overnight. As Rori talked about the dangers of bringing 'masculine energy' home into a relationship, I had an awakening (and I don't use that word lightly). As she spoke about the importance of being vulnerable and open, how we needed to stop chasing, managing, controlling and over-functioning, I could see myself in the reflection of her words.

I'll never forget the moment: there's a tick list in the book of characteristics that women wrongly think men crave in their ideal partner – someone who's smart, helpful, responsible, hardworking, successful, equal. The problem is, none of those connect to his heart. They describe a mate down the pub, a business partner or a woman he has a financial obligation to, not a receptive, creative, intuitive life partner who he feels safe with, nurtured by and genuinely connected to. This was a tricky one for me and seemed to go against everything I stood for and who I was, but I chose to consciously surrender to the process anyway, under the guise of this thought: 'If nothing changes, nothing changes'. Sometimes you need to be counterintuitive to what you expect, so you get a different result.

Part of the process is learning how to "be" rather than to constantly pursue. Rori uses the metaphor of a rowing boat. Imagine yourself in a rowboat with the person you love, floating in soft, calm water. Waiting for you at the shore is exactly what you want in your future. Who's rowing the boat? If it's you, how is all the extra effort affecting you? Is it making you angry, frustrated and exhausted? Why not put the oars down and float to the shore – let him take the lead for a while.

It's not about foregoing equality – it's about trust, balance and teamwork. By the time I'd finished the book, almost every page was covered in highlighter pen, scribbled notes and exclamation marks (this is me! it screamed). I felt like I'd been smacked in the face with my own truth. Just a few weeks after finishing the final chapter at home on a Friday night (that's how I roll), I met Jack at a speaking conference that he was organising. We shared the stage in five cities and by the third one, he asked me out for dinner and that was it. It turns out that while I'm a bit of a rebel in most aspects of my life, when it comes to relationships I could not be more traditional if I tried. I don't want bad boys who play mind games and take me on an adrenaline ride of highs and lows. I do want complete commitment, love and deep connectedness. That's just what works for me.

With Jack it was like coming home – comfortable, easy and effortless. In my old mindset, I would have been worried about writing so much about him in this book. It's like how they warn you not to get a tattoo of your boyfriend's name – what if it goes wrong, what if he leaves you? But do you know what? Although none of us know what the future holds, it's 100 per cent my intention to stand by him, and him by me, and so I'm willing to put that to paper. I could sit here and play 'what ifs' and get caught up in the statistics of how many relationships fail (in my own romantic past I've certainly added to them). But I knew from the start with Jack I didn't need to analyse, plan or forecast. He wasn't a project. Instead, he would be my equal other half.

When it comes to relationships people often go on about the importance of timing. Well, in theory, on paper, this was the absolute worst time for me to fall headlong in love. *The Collective* was in its infancy, I was under so much pressure, my team were practically sleeping at the office and my life was already bursting at the seams with commitments and responsibilities. But I firmly believe opportunities come at the right time, even though it might not seem that way. Jack brought me balance during the most stressful year of my career to date, which gave me added perspective and forced me to look beyond myself.

Most of my previous boyfriends didn't have a business background or an entrepreneurial bone in their bodies. I always convinced myself this was a good thing, because if we were both in that world we'd probably butt heads and be a nightmare (oh don't get me wrong – Jack and I have our moments). Now I realise this was all part of my 'top dog' syndrome. I was insecure, so I wanted to be the only one 'in the know' in the relationship. But Jack is a supremely successful, ambitious, talented and clever entrepreneur, and I love that about him. Every day he's constantly teaching me to be a better entrepreneur, without even realising, and I'm happy to learn from him. We support each other in a true partnership.

CTFO
(THAT'S CHILL THE F**K OUT)

Whenever a successful woman is interviewed in the media, they're often asked about 'the juggle', and how they cope with running a business, a partner and children if they have them. In a recent interview I was asked how many hours a night I sleep – there seems to be an assumption that all entrepreneurs suffer from insomnia. The interviewer seemed shocked when I admitted I always sleep for eight to 10 hours. Every night. Jack and I both do.

Recently, *The Collective* ran an article investigating the culture of 'sleep shaming' in the start-up community and how there's a weird glorification of sleep deprivation. Twitter founder Jack Dorsey works 16-hour days, sleeping only four hours a night, and still gets up at 5.30am to jog.

Yahoo CEO Marissa Mayer insists she needs only four to six hours sleep a night. Facebook CEO Sheryl Sandberg admitted in her book *Lean In* that she's been a slave to "competitive overworking" in the past. "My first six months at Facebook were really hard," she said. "A lot of the company followed Mark's [Zuckerberg] lead and worked night-owl engineering hours... I worried that leaving too early would make me stand out like a sore – and old – thumb. I missed dinner after dinner with my kids... I realised that if I didn't take control of the situation, my new job would prove unsustainable... I started forcing myself to leave the office at 5.30pm. Every competitive, type-A fibre of my being was screaming at me to stay, but unless I had a critical meeting, I walked out that door. And once I did it, I learned that I could."

I couldn't agree more – which might surprise you as I'm infamously driven and ambitious, but I've learned the hard way that burning out will not serve me. As an entrepreneur, for 13 years in business I made sure I was in the office by 8am. I felt I needed to beat my staff to their desks and set an example. Then I met Jack, who runs a big business with a large team, but still works from home generally about three days a week. He sets his own time schedule in a way Jack knows serves him, which does not mean leaping out of bed at dawn. If neither of us has a breakfast meeting, then we might stay at home and work.

We do not rush in the morning – which is a new concept for me – because I know that once I walk through my office door there will be no respite until I leave. In business mode, when we are on, we are on. With total tunnel vision and no distractions. So we make sure we have connected time together, outside our commitments. We call it 'CTFO', which stands for 'chill the f**k out'. Shall we CTFO tonight? We make a promise to each other to unplug from responsibility, relax and unwind.

Even though I often have events in the evening, when I'm not in the mood, when I crave alone time and know I need to go home and recharge, I am the queen of popping in and out if the function allows. I say hi to the right people and I'm off again, back to my cosy home, my trackie pants and a daggy show on the television. Jack and I are simple people in our downtime. When you're in love – yes I am, truly and infinitely – it doesn't take a lot of stuff, events or added excitement to be happy.

The author James Patterson once said, "Imagine life is a game in which you are juggling five balls. The balls are called work, family, health, friends and integrity. And you're keeping all of them in the air. But one day you finally come to understand that work is a rubber ball. If you drop it, it will bounce back. The other four balls … are made of glass. If you drop one of these, it will be irrevocably scuffed, nicked, perhaps even shattered."

That's why I'm wrapping my relationship in bubble wrap – not only does it offer protection from the outside world, but we can pop the bubble and have a good laugh together.

stretch yourself.

expand your heart

throw
L☮VE bombs
stop wars.

WHAT ARE YOUR PRIORITIES?

If I'm ever asked in an interview to put the different parts of my life in order of importance I say health is number one, then my relationship and then my business. This always seems to surprise people, as they assume that being a successful woman, business would come first. But that isn't the case anymore. If I'm not fit and healthy, then I can't maintain a good relationship, be a good boss or lead an inspiring community. And although creating cool stuff, having an impact on my community and fuelling a movement is amazing, when I look back on the really memorable moments of my life (with beautiful people in the world – friends, family, our readers), it's the times when I've had true human connection, like a birthday celebration for my mum, babysitting the boys (Jett and Banjo) for my beautiful friends Donna and Scott or just today, when a beautiful magazine reader looked me in the eye and said that they had launched a business after being inspired by myself and the team (incredible!). With Jack there are many, like the walk on the beach when we clambered over rocks with our dog Benny looking for a new adventure, and when we laughed our butts off when we went to Disneyland and he said, "I'll have two corndogs and a Coke – yep, I'm here to play" (see, you don't find that funny but we laughed and laughed because that's what you do when you're in love – you both think you are the funniest people on the planet). Business is just one part of the game. The real currency is true, human connection, which incidentally is why I created *The Collective* – to mesh the two.

I can broker multimillion-dollar deals. I thrive on the massive adrenaline rushes, the fist pumping and the power surges. But when I'm in that mode, I'm acting from a very masculine energy. For me personally, and I can only speak for myself, I don't want to bring that forcefulness home with me.

When I'm with Jack, I'm happy to not always be 'Lisa Messenger the businesswoman' (although we also have robust, philosophical, world-changing business conversations). I can take off my armour, snuggle in his arms and let him look after me, protect me and nurture me. Of course, our masculine and feminine roles flip sometimes between caretaker and receiver. As Rori Raye says, the man doesn't have to emanate masculine energy all the time, nor does the woman have to seep feminine. But it's not beneficial for you to both be in one category at the same time. Recently we had a crazy storm and water flooded our downstairs hallway. I was running around in a frenzy building dams out of towels and trying to salvage furniture, while Jack was lying on the bed upstairs laughing and being no help at all. But if we'd both panicked it would have been chaos, and his lack of concern was infectious. I ended up laughing too as I scrambled around like Noah trying to save him and Benny from the rising waters.

Another book I found very useful, and maybe you will too, is *The Five Love Languages* by Gary D Chapman (it's sold more than 9 million copies – that's a lot of couples who struggle to communicate). The premise is pretty simple but was a huge "wow" moment for me. In short, Gary argues there are five ways that people show love – words of affirmation, acts of service, receiving gifts, quality time and physical touch. It's important to respect your partner's preferred means of showing the L-word. For instance, you might think he's neglectful because he doesn't hold your hand walking along the road, but maybe that's just not his thing. Instead, he showers you in "acts of service" – to him fixing your car in the rain is just as romantic. Jack and I aren't really into gifts but for us, physical touch, words of affirmation and quality time are hugely important. This doesn't mean you have to find someone with a matching 'language', but just be aware the L-word is expressed in different forms, and the way you express love may not be the same way your partner does. Sometimes you both have to adapt.

I also revisit William F Farley's book *His Needs Her Needs* a lot (don't be put off by the tagline – 'Build an affair-proof marriage' – as I resonated with this book even when I was single). The author's theory is that love is a "learned association"

– if someone is present enough when you're feeling particularly good, the person's presence in general might be enough to trigger that good feeling (which becomes love). The skill is identifying, listening and observing what makes your partner truly happy, and then helping to replicate this. Simple really! Except many of us are too consumed in ourselves, and somehow miss the needs of our partners.

The reason I'm sharing these books (no, I'm not getting a cut of their royalties!) is that I openly admit that I don't personally have all the answers. I'm simply a very willing student, a guinea pig and ongoing experiment. I'm neither a dating guru nor a psychologist and neither is my relationship perfect (whose is?) although it does feel perfect for me. I know my journey is exactly that – my own – but the key takeaway here is that I wasn't too broken to be fixed nor was I too old (that sounds hideous doesn't it?) to learn. I wrote this chapter the day before Jack and I flew out to LA on holiday. I'd been planning to work on the 15-hour flight but instead grabbed my copy of *Have the Relationship You Want* on my way out of the door. Writing about love made me remember that it's an ongoing journey and it's important not to become complacent, to keep checking your agenda, your behaviour, your reactions. If you start a new fitness regime and hit your ideal weight or fastest time, you wouldn't expect to be able to stop exercising and still maintain those fitness levels. The same applies to nurturing relationships. You have to keep working at them and exploring them, keeping your heart open, light, bright, soft and sensual. I hope I'm just at the beginning of my journey. If you take anything from this chapter let it be this: love might not look like you imagine, it might not look like a movie or fit the template you think is acceptable. It might not be the fairytale you envisioned when you had your first kiss in a wool shed (or wherever you had your first lip lock), but I truly, truly believe there is someone out there for everyone. I love the advice that Huma Abedin, Hilary Clinton's deputy chief of staff, was given by her mother. "Take a chance. Don't be afraid of what you don't know. And don't fall in love with Plan A." I'm pretty sure she was talking about business, but I think it's a perfect attitude to love as well.

LOVE, BEYOND

Love doesn't just mean a bond between two life partners, or even friends or family members. One of my favourite videos from recent years is Tommy Franklin – aka 'the dancing man' – who first gained public attention when he was caught on video dancing on a sidewalk in Byron Bay in the rain, totally oblivious to passers-by, caught up in his own moment of joy and movement.

How many more of us could benefit from dancing as if no one was watching, from letting our happiness erupt, amplifying it and spreading it like a sunbeam? Why is it that if we see someone dancing in the street we think they're odd? If a stranger grins at us, our first reaction is often suspicion. What do they want? Why are they smiling at me? Yet, if a stranger stomps past us scowling and swearing under their breath, it's seen as perfectly normal.

There are entire generations and cultures where it's not okay to express feelings or say you love each other. Even among groups of women, admitting that you're really, really in love and really, really happy can be a faux pas – it's seen as being cheesy or boasting or tempting fate in case speaking it aloud makes it all go wrong. I have been guilty in the past of 'dealing in negativity', picking apart the world and only vocalising its flaws because I was wearing shades and could only see the shadows. That's why I make no apology for being happy now – I shout it from the rooftops – because I was so unhappy for so long. The old me wasn't much fun to be around when it came to relationships.

Make spreading love part of your purpose, in your home, your community, your social media feed and every corner of the world within your reach. Smile at a stranger, wave at a neighbour, send a handwritten thank you note to an acquaintance who has gone out of their way to help you, and hopefully we can start a domino effect and love, love, love together.

sacred

spaces

My mum often jokes that I am solar-powered. I can't stand not being able to see the sunshine in the daytime. It sends me into a spiral. When it's light outside I need to be beside a huge open window, or ideally, out in nature under the sky and in the fresh air. I can't go to a movie in the daytime unless it's storming outside – I can't bare the thought of all that lightness, that brightness, that radiance happening on the other side of a wall, behind a concrete ceiling, and that I'm not able to experience it.

That's why my home, my office, the hotels I stay in, the restaurants I eat at, the activities I plan, even the cars I drive are all chosen to facilitate my longing for luminescence. I don't know the reason behind this aversion, and I don't need to. I just recognise that I need constant doses of light to feel creative, alert, alive and to thrive. I also cannot work at all when certain types of symphony music are playing. I don't know why. Even if it's the most beautiful melody, it instantly flattens me, drains me and debilitates me.

However weird my triggers sound to you, it's my truth. Part of my journey from broken soul to confident, focused game-changer has been giving myself permission to recognise where and when I work best, when I'm most productive and switched on and shining, and then recreate those elements wherever I go.

Why am I telling you this? Because a lot of people underestimate the importance of their surroundings, and the huge knock-on effect this has on their ability to work, play, relax, thrive, connect and contribute. In *Daring & Disruptive,* I spoke about the mindset behind *The Collective* office and how I'd purposefully

designed it to feel like a home – soft, nurturing and feminine – rather than a grey, harsh, corporate cauldron. But when I mention 'sacred spaces' I'm not just talking about the place you work. Everyone needs a place where they feel they belong, whether it's a place to create a business, connect with friends, rest, relax, sleep, read or just be.

Where do you feel at your most optimum? What are the common factors in the places, spaces, environments and locations where you feel at your most invincible, grounded, rounded and vibrant? This is about growth and getting to know yourself, discovering your triggers – both positive and negative – and putting them to good use.

I want to be careful here not to go on and on about 'my way' because it's not necessarily the right way. My idea of a heavenly sacred space could be your idea of hell – and vice versa. It's a good thing my path never crossed with Roald Dahl's (although ironically his were some of my absolute favourite books growing up) because as far as creative spaces go, we are polar opposites. Apparently the author tried his best to block all natural light out of his writing hut – he preferred to work in a "tight, dark and warm" environment. That's not all! The table next to his desk was covered in keepsakes including part of his own hipbone, which he'd had removed, and a big ball of silver paper that he'd collected from bars of chocolate since he was a schoolboy. Who am I to judge? When you're a creative whose brainwaves are buzzing, whose imagination is flitting and who constantly shifts between the real and fantasy, it's important to have reminders of your past, your core, your sense of self. I get it! In each situation – dark or light – space is important to the creator's artistic process.

There is no set formula for creating a space that promotes productivity, contentment and energy. That's like expecting the same exercise plan or diet to work for every single body type! A happy space doesn't have to be this cool, calm oasis of Zen. It doesn't have to be a hyperactive, multicoloured explosion. Maybe it's something in between. It doesn't have to be expensive; you don't need a fancy

When it rains,
look for
rainbows.
When it's dark
look for stars.

— Anonymous

interior designer at your disposal. It could be as simple as opening a window so you can hear the wind rustling outside, adding pot plants and fresh flowers or investing in a chair that doesn't cramp you. I have a friend who runs a graphic design business and she does her best work when she sits cross-legged like a yoga instructor. So she sold her cramped office chair and bought a bench that has enough room to bend her legs around.

I get it. Not everyone has the luxury in their home of being able to have a separate office or a dedicated yoga room (I don't, although it's on my vision board when I next move), but a sacred space can be simple. Some of the most homely homes I've ever been in are the smallest spaces. Bigger isn't always better. Your sacred space could be symbolised by one cushion in your favourite colour. Tell your family, your friends, your colleagues; when I am sitting on this cushion I am having me-time, I am reconnecting, I do not want to be disturbed until it leaves my bottom. Create your own 'creative' island, put down roots and thrive on it!

GREAT MINDS, GREAT SPACES

The most important factor when creating a happy space is that it's totally, genuinely in line with your brand, purpose, values, likes, dislikes and attitude. When Bill Gates needs to recharge, he takes a 'think week' at a holiday house in a cedar forest in the Pacific Northwest, where he reads company reports and bans anyone from visiting, except for a caretaker who brings him two meals a day. Usually clam chowder and toasted cheese sandwiches, apparently. It's this magic formula, he's worked out, that fuels his personal epiphanies. But everyone is totally different.

Since launching my publishing business, and especially since starting *The Collective*, I've visited thousands upon thousands of offices, meeting clients, allies, competitors and investors. The two workspaces that have given me the most office-envy could not have been more different, totally at odds with each other's culture but equally inspiring to their inhabitants and to me as a visitor.

The first was Martha Stewart's office in New York. You walk into the foyer, which is plain, stark and non-descript, and then you walk through another door and it's like this huge reveal, entering a magical wonderland of white, crisp, clean, organised elegance. It's huge – like a mini village – but is segmented and compartmentalised, with one room full of flowers, another for crafting, another for cooking and an entire one filled with different types of cutlery, all neatly sorted and labelled. It's exactly what I imagine the inside of Martha's mind looks like – grounded, earthy and extraordinarily efficient. I wanted to live there. Indefinitely.

Then there's the other end of the scale. This year I visited the Las Vegas headquarters of the online apparel store Zappos, whose mission statement is 'to live and deliver WOW'. Well, their offices certainly reflected that. They're a chaotic explosion of colour, extravagance and celebration. Every employee is allowed to decorate their personal space in any way they desire, so every inch is totally different. There are party streamers hanging from the ceiling, blow-up toys, ping pong nets across desks and big blackboards covered in doodles. Okay, it isn't to my taste, but it perfectly suits their work culture of self-expression, freedom, being bigger, bolder and brasher than all their competitors. And their employees seem to be having the time of their lives – Zappos was ranked number 31 in *Fortune* magazine's annual 100 Best Companies To Work For list of 2013. They now even give public tours of their offices, offering a glimpse of life behind the doors at Zappos.

When creating a sacred space, different factors will be more important to different people – having an office close to home so you don't need to commute, good coffee nearby, a big-screen TV in the corner – we all have our preferences. That's why I'm not going to tell you exactly how to create a happy space.

Instead I'm asking you to ask yourself: where do you feel most comfortable and confident? Where do you laugh the loudest? Where do you let your guard down? Where do you feel the urge to take an Instagram photo because you want the world to see what you see and feel how you feel? Where do you get your biggest ideas? Where do you feel free to stretch your mind to the possibilities of life? Where do you ponder and question? Next time you have a big idea, an amazing day or a moment when everything just seems to fall into place, grab a notebook – or open the notes app on your phone – and write down where you are, what you see around you, what you can smell, hear, touch and even taste in the air. Then over time look for patterns in these happy places and recreate that habitat when you need a bit of a kick up the bum, a creative gee-up or to relight your inner fire.

Take time to notice your triggers, and then take time to transform your places and spaces to accommodate them. You'll know deep down exactly what elements you need to add or remove to feel nurtured, nestled, stimulated, encouraged or content. If you're struggling to find inspiration, purpose and passion, build it and they will come…

ON THE ROAD (AGAIN)

I'm writing this chapter from a one-star motel in a tiny country town, nine hours drive from Sydney. I agreed to meet Jack here to attend his friend's wedding (he's driving straight from a speaking gig in Melbourne), but things aren't exactly going to plan. That's an understatement.

You know those trips where everything goes wrong? I'll spare you the details but, to cut a long story short, due to a mix-up with the dates, the destination and the hotel booking, I'm currently sitting on a single bed (the only furniture in the room) with no sign of my partner and a phone that's run out of battery, after driving 900km on my own when I should really be back at the office because the magazine's about to go to press. Not ideal!

Now, I'm ALL for adventure but by this stage I'm tired, hungry and missing my team, my routine and my touchstones. So I started crying. Just a little bit. Then I soon got bored of that (well, there's no one here to comfort me!) and decided I had to shift my perspective. I looked around at my motel room – it was clean, it was comfortable, it was safe and it was my own space. I've certainly stayed in – and had fun in – a lot worse places.

I took some long, deep breaths and as soon as I shifted my mindset, the room instantly became a warming, welcoming environment. I ended up tracking down the local newsagent – the only newsagent in town – and having a lovely chat about *The Collective* with the woman who owned it. I left her a few copies so hopefully by now they're part of our movement! The moral of that story is it really is up to us to turn a negative into a positive. And a happy space can be any space – even when you're far, far from home.

I travel for my job – a lot. It's a personal choice. I believe that exploring new horizons, roaming, scouting, searching and seeking are a vital part of my job and hugely important in building a disruptive business.

explore,
roam,
scout,
search,
seek >>>

But all this wandering can come with downsides – travel can be unsettling, and I'm not just talking motion sickness.

I'm often asked how I remain so level-headed and seemingly unfazed even in the midst of a frantic business trip where my flight has been delayed, I've eaten nothing but complimentary peanuts for the past 12 hours, I have to check into the hotel then rush straight out to speak at a conference even though my suitcase has gotten lost and I have to go on stage in my track pants (unfortunately true story!).

Over the years, as I've become more experienced at travelling, I've developed strategies and patterns to keep me grounded wherever in the world I am. The first thing I do when I arrive at a new hotel is unpack my suitcase. In its entirety. Out come the clothes, shoes, beauty products, spare plugs, half-read magazines and the shrapnel from the bottom of my hand luggage.

I do not travel light. I do not apologise for this. In my home life I'm not a big fan of 'stuff' but I find that I need certain possessions to anchor me when I travel. When we arrived in LA and unpacked, Jack couldn't believe how many clothes I'd brought but I like to be prepared for every eventuality, so that I never have to wonder 'what if'. I unpack everything into neat, little piles, which grounds me and gives me a sense of place, attachment and belonging.

When I go on holiday, I bring a pile of books with me – real books, not the e-version, even though they weigh down my suitcase. To me, the smell and feel of a real book signals holiday time and nudges my brain into relaxation. I also carry around a LOT of mags – mine and other people's. It's one of the rare times I actually get to read them!

I always take my iPod, my Nikes and my gloves for weight training, which I do a lot when I'm away – I finally have time for it and it's one of my greatest passions. These all feel like home to me. I also take a photo of me and my grandfather – my greatest inspiration and mentor. He's been gone about five years but I never miss him because I feel him with me every single day, every single step

LIFE & LOVE

of the way in my journey. Until I'd experienced this, I would probably not have thought it possible.

If any of your prized possessions are travel-sized, why not bring them with you? My friend is a successful newspaper reporter and no matter where she goes on assignment – whether it's a city, a rainforest, a swamp or a war zone – she always packs a bright yellow china teapot, tea cup and saucer. When she gets writer's block she says the ritual of brewing tea and sipping it from 'her' cup helps. Anyone else might think it's silly. Her boyfriend does. But she has identified what works for her and she uses it to her advantage (that teapot has logged some serious air miles).

The travel companion you need to stay anchored might be a person – Richard Branson goes everywhere with his assistant Helen who he calls his "extra memory". It could be a soundtrack – Meg Whitman, CEO of Hewlett-Packard, can't live without her country music playlist. It could even be a colour – Dave Kerpen, CEO of Likeable Media, carries an orange backpack, orange pens, an orange phone cover and wears orange sneakers. It's not just because it matches the colour of his company logo. "The truth is I love the colour for how it makes me feel as a leader and how it affects others," he says. "I believe orange stands out in a positive way and makes people feel positive, energetic and full of hope."

Once again it comes back to finding out what works for you. Your body and mind know what they need to feel good, just as your body craves a certain food, but you have to listen, accommodate and appreciate it. You can create a happy, sacred, grounding space wherever you are. In a hotel room, in an airplane, in a taxi stuck in traffic on Hollywood Boulevard. You can wallpaper the walls with good intentions, carpet the floor with the right attitude and scatter rituals around like cushions, until any space is your space. Until you can be truly happy anywhere – even in a motel room, lost in the middle of nowhere.

She designed a life she loved

-Anonymous

ativity

Stay curious.
Stay creative.
Stay hungry.

Where are the places you get your inspiration from? I'm often seen sprinting out of the toilet in the office yelling, "I just had the best idea ever!" That's the throne where the real magic happens. I also have some of my greatest 'aha' moments in the shower, when I'm not distracted by people, emails and I can't check my iPhone. Constantly.

We've been conditioned from school to think that we're at our most productive when sitting at a desk. And maybe that is true for some people. But I find that it's not in meetings or scheduled brainstorming sessions where creativity really hits me and this is well documented of other creatives through history. It's the moments in between, when you give yourself space, freedom and flexibility to stop thinking so methodically, to stop trying so hard, and make room for ideas to arrive. I am a little bit obsessed with how other entrepreneurs, creatives, style makers and thought leaders get over the dreaded creative block – it happens to us all sometimes. Also, reading about other people's quirks makes me feel more relaxed about my own – and theirs. Did you know Benjamin Franklin started every day with an "air bath"? He'd sit for up to an hour naked in front of an open window in his house to get his mental juices flowing.

Doctor Yoshiro NakaMats – the man who patented the floppy disk (remember those?!) and more than 3377 other inventions – finds inspiration by diving deep into a swimming pool and staying there until his breath is about to run out. He believes his best ideas come just before his air is used up, when he jots them down on a waterproof notepad.

I'm not saying you have to become a nudist or free diver to find your mojo, but all of us, without exception, whether we're an entrepreneur, a parent, a spouse or all of the above, must ensure we don't get too trapped between four walls – we need to get out to fire up our senses. Even for a brief break to recharge.

When we can't get out, we need to ensure our place of creativity is actually creative! Anyone who's visited my office will know that my walls are covered – and I mean covered – in inspirational images I've ripped from books and magazines. My entire office is a vision board of the life I want to manifest; the places I dream of visiting, the quotes I want to live by, the mountains I want to metaphorically and literally climb.

But these pictures, ripped from books, old journals and magazines, are just reminders of where I want to be – they're not a replacement for actually visiting, touching, feeling and experiencing. They are the next step in my journey, in my learning. As I mentioned before, I recently read Richard Branson's book *The Virgin Way*, in which Richard talks about the stifling nature of the traditional education system. "The paradoxical twist is that ever since I dropped out of school," he says, "I have spent the balance of my life with a thirst for learning about new things, businesses, people and cultures. The big difference, of course, is that my learning process has involved experiencing all these things first-hand as opposed to reading about them in books or third-hand from someone who, frequently, had never lived outside of academia."

I didn't drop out of school (it probably would have tipped my parents over the edge, although my headmistress would have secretly championed it – or offered up a huge sigh of relief at the very least), but the education system never made sense to me, and certainly didn't inspire me. Not for a second. That's one reason why I never want my workspace to feel like a classroom. I've been to conferences where you are preached at for hours under fluorescent lights, while being suffocated by air conditioning and crippled by uncomfy chairs. While it might be fine for a while – or fine for some people for a long while – it's not for me.

I still go to a few conferences and seminars but I'm picky about the ones I'll attend (or my team attends) because I'd rather we all… got out, lived life, explored and stretched our collective imaginations on the job.

When I do attend, I do it my way. If sitting in an uncomfy chair isn't connecting me to the learning, I'll happily sit on the floor or cross-legged on a desk up the back, as long as I'm not throwing the organisers into complete turmoil because of my disruption. Someone recently said to me, "as long as no small children are in danger" they pretty much do what they want. It's not a bad philosophy.

LOOK, LISTEN, LEARN

It's easy to get caught up in the concept of 'uniqueness' and being original. But few ideas and creative brainwaves come from absolutely nowhere. Studies have shown the most creative people are those who see the world from different perspectives and have experienced different cultures, worldviews and extreme experiences. I couldn't agree more!

I've spoken about my love of travel, but you don't need to leave the country – or even your town – to spark a fire within you. I often take my team on excursions to look for inspiration. Recently, I took my design department out for a few hours in the bohemian backstreets of Newtown, Sydney. We spent the afternoon strolling around second-hand bookstores, looking at graffiti on the walls, the kooky people wandering by, soaking up the street life, colour and energy. At the end of the day, we went to an art store and I gave them a budget to spend on paper, pens, paints and ink stamps. The trip only took a few hours out of our day, but was the equivalent of a week's worth of browsing the Internet

Don't
grow
up.

It's a
trap.

—Anonymous

for inspiration and, some would say, much more effective. We touched, tasted, smelled and embraced every facet of the environment for maximum inspiration.

I often get emails from readers asking, "What's that handwriting font you use in the magazine?" Umm, I have absolutely no idea. One of my designers got a cool calligraphy pen (she has a whole repertoire these days) and started writing with it. It's a great, albeit simple example of creativity in action. Don't get stuck on a guidebook, draw outside the lines and create, replicate or develop your own style.

While we're on the subject of getting out and about, I have to say that I'm a big fan of walking. Anywhere. Everywhere. When I'm on holiday, I often just pull on my sneakers and walk for hours and hours, stumbling across different shops, cafés, looking at markets and street art. There are ideas everywhere if you open your eyes to them. I'm not the first creative to be at their most productive when pacing. Stanford University researchers found that a person's creative output increases by 60 per cent on average when they're walking.

Beethoven wrote symphonies while strolling alone through the vineyards of Vienna, British author Virginia Woolf would wander through London's parks and Steve Jobs was known to invite clients on a power walk. I am well known for conducting meetings while doing the famous Bondi to Bronte Beach walk in Sydney with my pup Benny in tow or taking a scheduled office meeting to the nearest park (again, with Benny by our sides).

Another benefit of our little team outings is that we all get to hang out together outside of the office. A few months ago, when the magazine hit its target and exceeded budget (woo hoo – a rare occurrence in its infancy!), I took my sales team to a day spa for massages, then out for sushi at one of the city's best Japanese restaurants, then out for ice-cream at one of Sydney's gelato institutions, known for, among other flavours, their milk chocolate with choc peanut fudge. We brought the biggest tub possible back to the office. It wasn't just about treating them but also inspiring them. We kept changing location for a reason. Every stop was a new sensory overload, and an opportunity for ideas, motivation and muses. It was also a chance for me to stop being 'just the boss' and hang out on the same level as my crew. We're a super close-knit team but it allowed them to feel even more comfortable and free with their suggestions and gave us some 'out of the office time' to really connect.

If you're feeling creatively stale, then shake it out, brush it off and get out of your box, which you probably created for yourself. I created *The Collective* as a starting point to awaken people's ideas and make them see past the tips of their noses. What I really hope is the magazine – and all that flows from it – will act as a springboard, a launch pad, a starting point.

That after you read our stories you will want to get out there and live, feel, touch and embrace all that you can for yourself.

Draw outside the lines.

Develop your
own style

And create with wild abandonment.

FREE UP YOUR FREE TIME

When I talk about creativity, it's not just about coming up with an amazing idea for a product or the latest reincarnation of your business. It can be about unleashing creativity in your everyday life, in your own little corner of the world, on your own level, at your own pace. This isn't about finding a creative business; it's about having a creative life.

Every week I meet people who say they're fed up with their nine to five jobs, but they can't leave because they feel tied to their mortgage, their responsibilities. I get it. We're grown-ups. But that's still not a reason not to pursue a passion, even if it's the cherry on the top of the cake of your life, rather than the main meal. This could just mean finding a hobby that lights you up and putting boundaries in place so you stick to the commitment. A few terms a year I go to an art class every Tuesday evening for one hour and it's non-negotiable. Me-time can often get put on the backburner when we're juggling responsibilities but it's so important.

Take a moment to think: who were you before the world told you who you should be? Before you felt weighed down by responsibilities, commitments and dependants, what did you do for fun? What activities lit you up and made you glow? It could be sketching a picture by the beach, going swimming, painting your toenails or just reading really trashy chick-lit.

I am not a parent and I understand that people have obligations, but even if you are and that means for this season of your life it's all go, go, go, then ask your partner for five minutes or an hour off for the pure indulgence of refuelling your bank of creativity. Some of the moments that fill our souls take barely any time. I'm a big fan of having a one-song dance party in my living room. Just stick on your favourite anthem (at the moment mine is 'I Like to Move It'. Don't ask!) and dance it out as if no one is watching.

Being a grown-up can be seriously overrated sometimes, so jump up and down on your bed. Go on. Try it! It's fast, it's free and it can remind you you're alive.

You also don't know where a new hobby might lead you. Okay, you may never be able to give up your day job (and you might never want to), but it could add an extra layer to your life that you never imagined. A friend's partner is by day a corporate bigwig and by night designs rocket ships (I don't really understand this, but it seems incredible to me). I have a friend who is a lawyer but also a DJ and recently met a guy who works in advertising but is a butcher in his spare time. Really! He couldn't find a good supplier of organic meat in his area so he set up his own business on the side. It doesn't make him a fortune but it fulfils him. You should see the way his eyes sparkle when he talks about it.

By the way, he's also struck up a deal with a local brewery. He gives them free meat and they give him free ale. I am a big believer in reciprocity and love this type of old-school trade-off.

You don't need to run your own business to have entrepreneurial aspirations, to live with the same pizazz, courage, ambitions and freedom. Real creativity isn't about designing a perfect product, inventing a world-changing gadget or sketching a masterpiece. It's about colouring outside the lines, filling your life with colour and painting a rainbow over your corner of the world.

comm

unity

Thanks to the rise of social media, the word 'community' is bandied about a lot these days, but what does it really mean? To me, it's all about the basic human need to belong. To feel part of something. To feel valued. To feel like you can contribute. It means taking responsibility for others and them taking responsibility for you.

Let me give you an example. I recently met a friend for juice in the city – she took the train from Bondi to see me. On the journey, she noticed a guy in his twenties holding onto the rail near the train doorway. From his cane, she could tell that he was visually impaired.

She told me she was interested in her own thought process: 'I think he might need help alighting. I should help him. Should I help him? Someone else will probably help him. What if he doesn't need my help? What if he's offended? What if I try to help him, but do it wrong?' All these thoughts flew through her head in a matter of seconds before she mentally kicked herself. It was a no-brainer! As a human being, seeing another human being in need, she had to offer her assistance.

And so, when they reached the last station on the line, she asked if he'd like a hand off the train and guided him along the platform and up the escalators. When I asked what they talked about, she said that was the most memorable thing – after he thanked her, they walked the rest of the way in silence, he didn't feel the need to keep commending her or apologise for needing a hand. They were just two strangers doing something not that extraordinary really – helping each other. What she'd seen as a huge deal and overanalysed in her mind was just a normal human act. Except, we live in such an isolated, self-serving world sometimes that she almost hadn't offered to help, because it felt so alien.

I am a big believer in small, selfless acts – but I see them as selfish really. That's because everyday acts of kindness – whether it's paying for someone's coffee, taking time to call a friend who needs cheering up or dishing out free copies of *The Collective* (which I do constantly) give you such a glow, such a sense of pride, that they actually feel quite hedonistic.

It wasn't that long ago in the corporate world when doing 'good' wasn't that cool. In the '80s (apparently) it was all about stomping over each other, stabbing people in the back, dog eat dog… But we don't have to be mean to keep others keen – we can spread good vibes and be just as attractive. As I get older, I am more and more concerned about nurturing a community around me, and happy to invest my time and energy into it – whether that's my friends, family, neighbourhood or further afield. Even that is a selfish unselfish act in a sense. Doesn't everyone yearn deep down for a sense of belonging?

When I was growing up, I certainly did – and still do. What I've noticed in life is, whether it's a religion, a sports team or a social media platform, people just want to feel part of something. For a good portion of my life I felt like an outcast, even when I was surrounded by people. I felt different, disconnected or like the black sheep of my friendship group or family. I think a lot of entrepreneurs and creatives feel this way, as they seem to have visions that nobody else can see. I was always searching for a safe place or a sense of home, but the problem was I didn't have a clear vision of my own values. How could I expect to find, attract and keep a tribe who shared my common interests when I didn't know what they were yet?

I get high on intelligent conversations

-Anonymous

BRIDGE, BRIDGE, BRIDGE

As Mother Theresa said, "I alone cannot change the world, but I can cast a stone across the waters to create many ripples." It's something amazing to aspire to, isn't it?

When a friend of mine was eight months pregnant, a single guy from her church who had very little money and no family of his own went out of his way to go out and buy her dinner and deliver it to her house. He asked nothing in return, both then and since. She has told me that story many times and says she'll never forget the kindness.

I recently read a similar story from England. In one of the London newspapers, a journalist had been writing a column about her husband, who after a car accident had been in hospital for over a year recovering from a brain injury. One week she wrote about how he'd been moved to a different hospital, which had a pub across the road where she hoped he'd be well enough to visit one day. A week later, she discovered that a complete stranger had read that article, tracked down the pub and sent £10 to pay for their first drink. I love this on two levels: firstly for the small act of kindness, but also because that stranger is manifesting a miracle. Although her husband isn't well enough to go yet, the stranger believes that one day he will be.

I fully believe that a sense of community, and the power of a group of humans with a common purpose, can overcome many of life's hurdles. On an amplified scale, look at the power of the hashtag #illridewithyou after the terrible siege in Sydney's Martin Place in 2014. Despite the tragedy, commuters rallied to say they'd stand by Muslim Australians who feared a backlash on public transport.

We witnessed it bring so many people together across race, creed and religion. And it put Australia squarely on the map as a place of love and peace, which subsequently became so much bigger than the story on fear.

Do you walk around with blinkers on, or with your eyes wide open? Would you have noticed a blind man in the corner of the train, or would you have walked straight past him? I'm not saying this to be judgemental; I've suffered from 'kindness blindness' in the past. But helping others is a habit that we all should practice – because one day you might need help, too.

I have a quote from the novel *Second Glance* by Jodi Picoult pinned to my noticeboard above my desk that says: "Heroes didn't leap tall buildings or stop bullets with an outstretched hand; they didn't wear boots and capes. They bled, and they bruised, and their superpowers were as simple as listening, or loving. Heroes were ordinary people who knew that even if their own lives were impossibly knotted, they could untangle someone else's. And maybe that one act could lead someone to rescue you right back."

THE COLLECTIVE COMMUNITY

My mum and sister live in the hinterland of Byron Bay in Bangalow, a town with a population of less than 2000 people and only one newsagent. My family are so passionate about the magazine, they're always happy to be pulled into my bizarre experiments to see how we can stretch its reach, its message and its traction. One day they decided to do a little test. They collected the magazines that hadn't sold that month from the newsagent – there were only 17 left – and dropped them off at the local hairdressers, dentists and doctors to put in their waiting rooms. The hope was that local people would see it, read it, love it and next time, buy it (they've done this every month since).

Within two months, that tiny little Bangalow newsagent became the second-biggest selling newsagent of *The Collective* in the whole of Australia, not including airports. To put it in perspective, that's out of more than 3500 stores. This was a local shop in a backwater, but pretty special, town. It was extraordinary that my mum and sister could have that much impact on their own, just from spreading less than 20 free copies. It is proof that community amplification can happen in the most unexpected places.

I launched *The Collective* on March 4, 2013, knowing absolutely nothing about the industry – and I mean nothing. When I say I didn't have an ounce of experience in the field, I'm not exaggerating. But I did have a crystal clear vision. *The Collective* has really strong "anything's possible", inspiring and motivating messaging. It's filled with the real-life stories behind the stories, authentic voices, and the spin and hype are stripped back so it's attainable and relatable – people love that. I have always said I am just the conduit, just the architect providing the platform. Really, it is owned by our community, so we have enabled and empowered people to carry the message, to feel a part of it, to belong and be heard.

When we launched the first issue, we had a limited community at the time and nobody really knew who I was (many still don't), as I was solely publishing books for others that weren't about building a profile for myself. Fast-forward 18 months, and we're now sold in more than 35 countries and 3500 newsagents in Australia alone. We're in every domestic Virgin and Emirates lounge and every single domestic and international Qantas Chairman's, Club and Business lounges. We're ranged in Australia's biggest supermarkets. We're in all 700+ Barnes & Noble stores in the US. We are building to be absolutely everywhere! Although we still have plenty of room to grow, I now know in every cell of my body the power of community, because I could never have done it without you, you, you and you.

I recently shared in the magazine the moment when I knew, without doubt, that *The Collective* community was fulfilling its purpose. It was when I clicked onto

Instagram and read a series of messages between readers that filled my heart with pride, gave me goose bumps and brought tears to my eyes.

It all started under a photo I'd posted of a diary we produced for our readers. In the comments, a reader called Lucy had written, "Lisa, I ordered three diaries but have been sent five. What would you like me to do with the additional ones?" I told her to keep them – a gift from us to her – and that's when the magic started.

Lucy asked if anyone else on our Instagram would like one of the spare diaries – for free. Her only condition was that whoever received the bundle of joy should 'pay it forward' by doing a good deed for another person.

It's funny how a simple act of generosity can be a beacon, catching the attention of everyone in the vicinity. Suddenly my Instagram feed became a marketplace for good vibes, as strangers traded #collectiveactsofkindness. A reader called Jasmine was sent a diary. It turns out she's an artist who, the day before, had donated a painting to a children's hospice. Oh karma, you are a clever seamstress!

One follower said she was moving overseas and had worldly belongings to recycle, upcycle and rehome if anyone would like second-hand books, furniture or kitchen equipment. We all know that social media can be a fickle and jealous battlefield, but here was proof the technology could be used to spread wonder, generosity and gratitude. When you give without expectation, when profit isn't always your end goal, you might find unexpected rewards that surprise you.

It perfectly summed up *The Collective*'s reason for being – to bring together like-minded people who want to make an impact in some way, to remind them everyone does have power and can be game changers. Each and every one of us. Every time *The Collective* kicks to another level, every time I say on social media that we've just been stocked in another country or that we've just heard we've sold out in a certain newsagents, I keep waiting to see if there's going to be a backlash, people looking to cut us down (that damn tall poppy syndrome!). But actually, people can't wait to rejoice with us, to share in our victories and start a Mexican wave of congratulations. Which is wonderful because really, where would *The Collective* be – where would we all be – without each other? I've always believed there is no such thing as a stranger, but this is a wonderful reminder. Let's make friends and influence people together!

FOLLOW YOUR LEADER

Not everyone wants to lead an army. I realise that. Creating a movement can mean a community of 5 million people, or 50 or just five. It really isn't about numbers, even though social media tries to tell us otherwise. It's about having a positive impact on those lives you touch, whether that's the shop assistant you smile at, the customer whose life you make easier with your product, or the stranger you buy coffee for with a 'kindness card' (if you haven't heard of them then Google the 'Wakeup Project'). Just make sure you're living your best life and usually like will attract like, if you lead by example. Still, building a community or even being part of one does take some effort, especially if you want your people to know you value them and their input. A lot of people are shocked that I handle all of my personal social media platforms, rather than hiring someone else to do it. I can't promise this will always be the case but I'll hold on as long as I can. I make an effort to reply to emails personally, whether it's from an important client or a reader, and I reply to Instagram comments, dole out likes and generally immerse myself in the chatter. Why wouldn't I reply to everything myself when my name – and mind and heart – is attached to it? If you were to spy on me mid-social sesh, you'd find daggy old me hanging out at home in my ripped jeans and thongs, checking my social media as I curl up with Benny.

Side note: if you're not currently proud of the person you are, then just be extra careful with your public platform. I'm so glad social media wasn't around when I was a lost soul. It makes me cringe to think about it. I was always saying the wrong thing, drink-dialling and regretting it. That was back in the day when you could only reach out to the people in your phone book, not the entire world with the click of a button.

Now it's different, as everything I speak, type, tweet and like is purposeful and considered. Through the work I've done on myself, I can now clearly speak my mind, stand up for what I believe in and unapologetically say that I want to do good in the world. Now I'm unashamedly myself in any situation. I'm who I am inside and out, I don't put on a mask, and that seems to draw people to me. This book isn't about being small and keeping yourself hidden, it's about shining and amplifying your message to the world.

But enough about me (for a moment). I've always said with *The Collective*, the brand is owned by the readers, the society, the movement. That feeling of shared ownership is ultra important when building a community. I really am just the conduit for change, and I've never been interested in creating a guru model. My mum and sister would never have bothered investing their time and energy touting those magazines around dentists, doctors and hairdressers in Bangalow if I hadn't made them feel invested in the magazine and its future. They, like all our readers, are as much a part of it as I am.

My role is just to be a magnet, and I think that's what great leaders do well – draw like-minded action-takers together. It's easy when you have a clear "why". What I've discovered, especially since launching *The Collective*, is that when you're fuelled by purpose and believe in yourself, everyone else starts to believe in you, to gravitate towards you and wants to be near you. A true sense of self is magnetic. For many years, before I started to explore personal development, spirituality and rediscover myself, I was a 'social chameleon', changing the colour of my personality to fit in with the crowd of people I was with at the time. There would be the Lisa I was at home, the Lisa I was at the office, the Lisa I was around my party friends, the Lisa I was around my parents. Of course, the problem with having split characters is you have to keep all the corners of your life separate. I didn't realise that the only way I'd find the right community for myself, the only way I'd discover that holy grail of 'belongingness', was to be myself, warts and all, loud and proud.

I've learned with *The Collective* that if you do something with the right intention and it's not all about money, but empowering people, then you just have to sow the seed and the community will run with it. After the success of the Bangalow experiment, we came up with the idea of starting an 'ambassador program'. We now have hundreds of ambassadors – they aren't famous faces with big profiles, but real readers of the magazine across Australia and around the world who really, truly adore the brand, and who we recruit to help us amplify our message. Every issue we give them a set of challenges – it might be as simple as sharing our cover on social media in a unique and interesting way. In exchange, we gift them tickets to cool events or send them surprise care-packages in the mail – it might be the candle we created with Palm Beach Collection or a box of Thankyou muesli (an amazing social enterprise I love to support, as profits from products sold go to fund water and health projects in the developing world).

We give them 'ambassador' logos to add to their email signatures and generally go out of our way to make them feel part of the team, valued and special – because they are! It could backfire, as we haven't actually met many of our ambassadors in the flesh, although we try to screen them as best we can to check their values line up with our own. I'm sure some big bosses would say that I'm mad because their messaging is so hard to control. But these are people who were already shouting about *The Collective* from the rooftops, even before we gave them an incentive. I truly believe that if people inherently want to help you anyway, you should reward them, trust them and let them rise to the responsibility. Most people love feeling part of something, on an equal footing and not less then everyone else in the community or movement. If you have a guru model set up to worship the leader, it's not going to work long-term and be sustainable – people soon get sick of being preached to. But if you make people feel just as important as the creator, then it will grow, expand, flourish and be a platform for liberation, love and acceptance.

Building a community is all about give and take, leading and being led, teaching and learning from each other. When it comes to control it's about balance; hold it too tight and it'll be crushed, hold it too loose and it'll fly away.

SOCIAL MEDIA

Thanks to the Internet, travel, television, Skype and social media, a community isn't confined to geographic boundaries. The whole world can be your neighbour, you can tweet a stranger 15,000km away for a cup of sugar (although it might take a while to get to you). There are really no limitations to who you touch, inspire, serve and share your resources with. It doesn't matter whether you're the head of a multimillion-dollar business, a new mother who's just discovered the best way to put her baby to sleep, or a fashion blogger sitting in her bedroom, whose boyfriend takes a photo of her outfit every day.

I'll never forget when my team and I sat down to brainstorm a cover star for Issue Seven of *The Collective*, and someone suggested fashion blogger Nicole Warne. I have to admit my first response was, "shouldn't we get someone who's actually famous?" Haha, how naive of me! Not only does the blogger behind Gary Pepper have more than 1.1 million Instagram followers, but hundreds of thousands of likes on Facebook at the time of print; it's now, no doubt, even more. When I searched for her name on Twitter, fans in Paris, Milan and London were calling her the greatest style icon who ever lived. This was, at the time, a 25-year-old girl who lived on the central coast of New South Wales (it's pretty small for those who aren't familiar with it), and until 12 months before we met, had rarely travelled and was yet to make her mark in the fashion industry. I was honoured when she agreed to be our cover star, and it was a poignant, teaching moment. It doesn't matter how much experience you have, whether or not your great-grandfather was someone special, or whether or not you have a big advertising budget. If you're authentic, open and clever about spreading your message, anyone can create a movement with no boundaries.

This will make me sound ancient, but when I was growing up there wasn't even a computer in our school, and if you wanted to access information you had to flick through the huge, dusty Encyclopaedia Britannica in the tiny, pokey library. If you were building a brand back then or wanted to share your product with the world, you had to either use traditional media channels – begging publications to feature you – send customers a letter in the mail or knock on every single front door. How wonderful is it that now anyone with access to a computer can stand a chance of creating something that reaches far beyond their immediate location. The power of social media is truly amazing to me, although I'm no expert and I'm still exploring, experimenting and learning. I'm just a novice compared to the game changers we've interviewed in *The Collective* who use social media for momentous social impact, from the Movember boys to the ALS Ice Bucket Challenge and hashtag campaigns aimed at empowering women like #leanin and #girlsrising.

It's all about creating unity, reducing feelings of isolation and loneliness. A recent study by The Dartmouth Institute for Health Policy & Clinical Practice found that people suffering from severe mental illness use YouTube to feel less alone, to find hope, to support and defend each other, and to share personal stories and strategies for dealing with the challenges of the everyday. But it doesn't have to all be heavy. You can build a community without a big, worthy cause behind you or a drive to change the world and save humanity.

WHO DOESN'T LOVE A CAT VIDEO?

When it comes to social media, I try not to take myself too seriously. I may be a business leader but I'm not exactly Nelson Mandela, and I want my Instagram feed to reflect my goofy, soppy, sentimental mash-up of a personality. A few nights before writing this chapter, I posted a photograph of two cats having a cuddle. I remember saying to my partner Jack at the time, "You just watch this go." As predicted, it went nuts – hundreds of likes in less than five minutes and a whole heap of regrams and comments.

It reminded me that the message you spread doesn't have to be some complicated, ground-breaking, death-defying announcement. It can be two cats cuddling that put a smile on someone's face (nobody is too cool for a cat video). It could be a trend that gets people moving, dancing, enjoying, and strips away their inhibitions (did you do the Harlem Shake?).

Recently, *The Collective* interviewed Erika Geraerts, Jess Hatzis and Bree Johnson, who are the founders of Frank – a natural body scrub. They created a fictional character to be the face of their product: a cheeky, sleazy, flirty guy called Frank, who flirts with customers on social media. "Hey babe, want me to scrub your back?" He even has a blog where he offers tongue-in-cheek advice on "how to make your bum more bootylicious". That simple bag scrub is now so coveted that in less than a year, sales have exploded across Australia and into New Zealand, the US and Europe.

A movement can be based on a shared joke or love of an unusual hobby. A list of the richest YouTube stars of 2013 includes EvantubeHD (an eight-year-old boy who reviews toys), BlueXephos (two video gamers obsessed with Minecraft and World of Warcraft), and PrankvsPrank (a girlfriend and boyfriend who play tricks on each other, which started after Jesse Wellens tricked his girlfriend into eating a spoonful of cinnamon).

None of these ideas are going to end world hunger, and yet they might just add a little bit of sunshine, laughter, knowledge or interest to a stranger's day, and therefore the movement they're building is just as valid. They're also driven by the creators' genuine interests. Do you play computer games? Talk about it. Do you collect miniature china kitten figurines? Well, there's probably someone out there somewhere who shares your passion, so connect with them.

My only rule for social media is the photos, quotes, sayings or regrams I post have to genuinely reflect the real me – although even I get it wrong sometimes and have to check myself. Not so long ago I was at a glitzy, fancy event to promote a glitzy, fancy car. I took a photo of myself posing across the bonnet and posted it on Instagram. Then five minutes later I deleted it, despite the fact it had got a lot of likes from car fans, and even a regram from a famous reality TV star. It may have got a lot of attention, but it didn't feel like 'me'. My only requirement in a car is that it's big enough to hold my surfboard and that the upholstery is dog friendly. Although growing a movement is important to further your causes, build a platform and get attention, don't let it mean you lose yourself and turn your back on your values. Don't sell out to get instant gratification. It might get you a lot of likes in the short term, but if you're sending out mixed messages, will your followers really feel loyal to you?

It's also important not to grow a movement on judgement or alienating others. I was at an event recently and was approached by a woman who has launched the first all-female company of electricians in Australia. She wanted my advice on getting publicity, and asked if I thought she should put out a press release claiming that women don't want male electricians in their homes as they don't feel safe. Hell no! It might get a few headlines in the papers, but it would be a short-term fix, with longer, negative consequences. She'd make enemies of every big, burly, male electrician in the industry.

In my experience, you're better off fostering positive relationships with your community – and even your competitors – to work together. Share your contacts, help each other and, if you're worried about people catching up or overtaking you, just move faster.

I don't use *The Collective*'s community to spread gossip, scaremonger, be salacious or complain about the fact my online shopping order is late or my local café messed up my lunch (seriously, first world problems!). It's not about living in a fantasy world or ignoring the bad stuff. It's about refocusing our energy on what we can change, and how we can uplift each other's spirits. We do talk about the good stuff and the bad stuff respectfully because both exist – we ran a recent article on the devastating journey of an entrepreneur who had to close her start-up and admit that the "big" dream hadn't worked, and our community is much stronger for it.

Better to be the one who smiled than the one who didn't smile back.

– Anonymous

style

Break the rules.
Stand apart.
Ignore your head.
Follow your heart.

I n the second year of *The Collective* I decided to shake-up our cover stars a little. You have to try something new, test out unchartered waters and take risks to keep things fresh in this game. Also, I have a short attention span, so churning out same-same covers just doesn't appeal to me. For our 16th issue, we decided to celebrate the new celebs of the cultural scene – fashion bloggers – with a cover shot of a group of the biggest-name bloggers. But instead of dressing them, we literally drew illustrations of outfits onto them. Cool, hey?

The end result was awesome. Our loyal fans, who never miss an issue, loved it, and we caught the eye of a whole new set of readers. Fashion lovers who eat, sleep, dream and live clothes. A lot of them reached out to me on Instagram, which it seems is the favourite social media hangout for stylish people, and started commenting under my photos on my outfits. It's flattering – but also pretty hilarious – as throughout my life I've never worn what I'm supposed to, what counts as 'fashionable' or what society dictates.

I'm sure I've broken every rule in the book, both in my personal style (pink and red, horizontal stripes) and also the clothes I've worn to business meetings (ripped jeans and Chucks while everyone else is suited and booted). I thought twice about including a 'Style' chapter in this book for that exact reason – I am no fashion icon! But this goes deeper than an aesthetic, 'look how pretty we are' level. I'm not going to tell you where to shop, what to wear or what not to.

Your look, your style, your image is another pillar in the all-important B-word: branding. Your purpose in the world, your chosen mission and goals, should flow through every aspect of your life, whether it's your appearance, your home or how you represent yourself on social media. If you meet someone who says they're highly organised, but then their house is full of clutter, the messages they're sending into the world are at odds and totally incongruent with who they are.

Look down at yourself right now. Yes, right now. What are you wearing? Take in every tiny detail, from the colour of your toenails if they're painted, to your accessories, your bag, your clothes and your hairstyle. You're a walking-talking billboard for your own life purpose, and what is yours saying? If it isn't aligned with the 'why' in your life then maybe it's time to give yourself permission to dress for your own song.

It's easy to get caught up in 'shoulds' when it comes to style. What should a successful entrepreneur, a good mother, a loving partner look like? How should we dress to fit into each of these categories? My dear friend Lorna Jane Clarkson – the cover star for the first-ever issue of *The Collective* – wrote in her book about how, when she first launched her active wear brand, she used to wear suits to business meetings and it left her feeling stiff, stilted and uncomfortable. Then one day she woke up and realised she wasn't being authentic. Off went the suits, on went her running pants… and she's never looked back.

Recently, when my partner Jack and I were on holiday in the Bahamas, it was really brought home to me how conditioned we are to dressing for other people's expectations. We were staying at this amazing resort, where I noticed a lot of businessmen were holding meetings. Good on them for that – sitting by a pool beats meeting in an office. But the thing is, they'd come to this amazing space by a pool surrounded by palm trees with the sun beating down… and they were all wearing suits. I was sweating in a bikini so they must have been melting. If only just one of them had said, "Why don't we all wear our board shorts?" then I bet the others would have jumped at it, but it takes a lot of courage to be the one to jump out of the box first.

I'm active and sporty, so often I will have a meeting in my training gear because self confidence is the best outfit. Rock it own it.

-Anonymous

it's what my life is about. I don't mean a sweaty, smelly sports kit – I have my limits. But if I'm walking my dog Benny in between meetings, I want clothes that I'm comfortable power walking around the park in. I make no apology for this as it's who I am, and it shouldn't come as a surprise to anyone who knows me, either in the real world or on social media.

When I arrive at a speaking gig in black leggings, this isn't a mistake. I didn't forget to pick up my suit from the dry cleaners. I'm wearing this because I've chosen to be me – in my business, in my brand, in every corner of my life. Everything I say, every word I write and everything I wear is purposefully, unapologetically on brand.

It all screams, "I am a rebel, I am doing this my way." I don't use clothes to hide my true self behind. I use clothes to amplify my message. To yell, scream and add colour to the purpose that I'm already projecting. If I started wearing a suit people would get mixed messages.

On the flip side, I'm not saying that every business meeting should be full of entrepreneurs in track pants. If you feel at your most productive, aware, reactive and vibrant when you're dressed in a suit, or a ball gown for that matter, then go for it. It's funny how, since Mark Zuckerberg burst onto the scene, much of Silicon Valley has adopted a 'grey hoody and sneakers' dress code. I wonder if there are techies there who think, "If only I could wear a suit and tie to work" but don't want to step out of line.

When people first start out on a new pathway – whether it's a new relationship, moving to a new city or a new business venture – it can be easy to fall into the pit of pretending to be another person to fit in. I've seen it a lot in entrepreneurs who are launching their own business and I have been there, too. It's a subconscious, natural tendency, and when you look back on it, it's often about a lack of confidence, naivety and the basic human need for acceptance.

The other day I was watching a video of Jack, who is a serial entrepreneur and one of the smartest businessmen I know. In this video, which was made four or five years ago, he is wearing a suit and looks as if he is attending a funeral. I started laughing because that's so at odds with the person he is today. But at the time he was finding his feet, still finding himself, still crawling out of the corporate chrysalis. I love seeing new entrepreneurs becoming more comfortable in their own skin and watching their brand, their style, their 'billboard' going from grey to a multicoloured spectacle.

This can be metaphorical. It doesn't mean you have to dress in a mishmash of fluorescent patterns (unless you want to). I recently had a huge wardrobe cleanout and donated my most colourful clothing to charity, because I decided my personal brand should be mainly about denim, leather, black, white and metallic – partly because I'm sartorially lazy and this means that anything I pull out of my closet with my eyes half closed in the morning will match. But also because it makes me feel confident and daring.

You can still wear black, but because it's your personal choice, rather than a restrictive dress code, your personality can project a rainbow.

Don't be afraid of being different.

Be afraid of being the same. ♡

DOES IT ALL MATCH ?

We all know deep down if we're faking it. We know if we're pretending to be someone else, if our inside doesn't match our outside, if our style doesn't reflect our purpose. As we wait at a train station, feeling uncomfortable in the high heels we didn't really want to wear but felt we should to impress a client, and spot the girl in the floaty linen dress and sandals, sitting crossed-legged on a bench looking light, bright, cool and composed, we have a moment of... I don't like the word envy, so let's say 'reflection'. We should have listened to our gut instinct, which told us to wear the outfit that makes us feel like we can dance, rather than the one that makes us feel caged.

I was talking about this chapter with my book editor Amy, who used to be the editor of *Grazia* Australia in her "previous life", as she calls it. She won't mind me saying – she doesn't exactly fit the mould of fashion editor (that's one reason why I love her). The Amy I know turns up to business meetings in trainers, carrying her skateboard and with feathers in her hair. But it wasn't always that way.

At *Grazia*, she dressed for everyone else but herself. She's pretty honest about it and says she was simply young and unconfident. As a result, she wore what she thought a fashion editor should wear, even though it was totally at odds with her personality. Amy's wake-up call came at a Melbourne Cup two years ago when she was judging the Ladies Day competition, Fashions on the Field. "I was dressed in a Chanel, pastel tweed suit," she tells me, at which point I'm laughing in disbelief.

"Everyone said it was amazing – and it was. For a women 20 years older. Not a 26-year-old who likes to be able to move, to bounce, to run." In that moment she realised things were far from right in her world. "I had to tap back into me," she says. I love that she had the courage to do it, retaining just as much professional swagger as she had while donning a tweed.

That being said, we don't all need to run around in yoga wear like a bunch of free-spirited hippies. My sister lives in the hinterland in Byron Bay and this is a topic we often discuss. The irony is that people often flee to Byron Bay – known for its relaxed vibe, concentration of hippies and all that is associated with that type of lifestyle – to leave convention and the corporate world behind, be liberated and find themselves.

But they then quickly adopt the 'Byron Bay uniform'. Harem pants. Prayer Beads. Crystals around their necks. Even unconventionality can become conventional sometimes. People yearn to belong, to feel united and fit in but don't be afraid to keep standing out and be yourself. If the real you wears a suit that's fantastic. If the real you wears ripped jeans and a logo T-shirt then go for it. Just because you work in a bank it doesn't mean you have to dress head to toe like a stereotypical banker – I have no time for stereotypes or status quo! Break out of the box, and you will feel better, more confident and able to tread your own path.

You might be reading this thinking, "It's okay for her. She runs her own business. No one will tell her off for flouting the dress code." You have a point. When you're the boss of your own business you can dictate the rules, although there are no rules in *The Collective* office, and my team wear a stunning cocktail of training gear, high fashion and denim. I appreciate that I'm in the fortunate position of being able to dress any way I choose, and that some companies do have guidelines you need to work within. If you're in a customer-facing job, it might not be acceptable to sit behind your desk in training gear, but dressing for you doesn't have to be that extreme. How can you add small elements of 'you' to your wardrobe – a statement bracelet, pink toenails, maybe a kickarse handbag with metal studs or a pair of leopard-print socks? Whatever works for you, whatever makes you smile when you see a flash of it in the mirror. You might not be able to 'be you' from head to toe, but everyone can include a sneaky hint of what they are in their outfits, something that acts as a touchstone, a reminder that you are more than what the world dictates you 'should' be.

When she transformed
into a butterfly, the
caterpillars spoke not of
her beauty, but of her
weirdness.

They wanted her to
change back into what
she always had been.

But she had wings.

— Dean Jackson

YOU'RE WEIRD...
UNTIL YOU'RE COOL

The whole concept of coolness is something I'm fascinated by, and have debated into the night with my friends, my sister, anyone who'll listen. My whole life I've been a little weird; from the clothes I've worn to the odd rituals I do and the jokes I find funny. I think I am deeply uncool and I'm unapologetic about it.

But then this weird thing happened. Before I started *The Collective* – when I was just Lisa as opposed to 'Lisa the editor of a magazine' – people took little notice and probably laughed at me more than with me. But now that I have a semi-profile, their attitude is shifting. Like a lot, well at least to my face and across social media. I have a theory: when nobody knows who you are, your oddities and wacky habits are just weird. But once you become a person of some status and have a public platform, suddenly your eccentricities are acceptable. Suddenly they're actually cool! This amuses me. Greatly.

I like to use the example of pop stars with crazy demands that we hear about from time to time – those who will only eat red M&M'S or drink water chilled to an exact temperature. If an average Joe made these demands they'd be laughed out of town, but when a person deemed as 'famous', with more than 100,000 Twitter fans and a team of personal assistants does it, suddenly it's justifiable. In fact, fans even start to copy it – look at the cult who follow celebrities' weird diets. Isn't that a bit scary? Note to self and anyone reading: do not become a dickhead if you get some level of success and notoriety.

I've never really tried to hide my weirdness because it takes far too much energy, but these days I'm really embracing and enlarging it, and I am proud of it. Now that I've created a platform for myself, through *The Collective* and in building my own profile, I've discovered I can be really crazy and naughty, speak my mind for good, buck the status quo and what's accepted as the norm, and people actually celebrate it. In one of my editor's letters I shared a story that proved this. I was at a big corporate lunch and there were 16 CEOs all banging on about what pains Gen Ys were. I bit my tongue, waiting for the right moment, and then lobbied my counter-argument. "I'm not a Gen Y but I'm doing my best to adopt their traits, their go-getting mentality and fierce confidence."

Well, suddenly I had 15 people agreeing with me. It was staggering to see how quickly the entire room's opinion shifted. So often people are sheep, they follow the crowd for fear of ridicule. But if you are strong and courageous enough to speak your mind and back it up, suddenly people will start agreeing with you. This provides an extraordinary opportunity if you are a good, well-intentioned person with a big platform to make some serious change in this world.

The reason I'm bringing this up is not to show how important I've become (yeah, right!) but to put into perspective just how ridiculous the concept of coolness is. To remind us all why fitting in really, really doesn't matter. The carousel of coolness will spin, sometimes you're riding high and sometimes you're the lowest of the low. Whatever! My message: keep being weird, keep embracing your quirky, funny, wacky ways and maybe someday it will turn around and you'll be cool. Maybe you won't. Who really cares? That's right, no one.

I adore the wording that Steve Jobs used in an Apple campaign. It makes my heart leap every time I hear it or read it. As soon as you read it, you'll know why: "Here's to the crazy ones – the misfits, the rebels, the troublemakers, the round pegs in the square holes. The ones who see things differently. They're not fond of rules and they have no respect for the status quo. You can quote them, disagree with them, glorify them or vilify them. About the only thing you can't do is ignore them because they change things. They imagine. They invent. They heal. They explore. They create. They inspire. They push the human race forward... And while some may see them as the crazy ones, we see genius. Because the people crazy enough to think they can change the world, are the ones who do."

role ma

&

'wou'

dels

moments

why stop dreamy

when you wake up?

– Anonymous

've had many 'wow' moments in the past year, but one of the most jaw-dropping ones was sitting on a sofa next to Sir Richard Branson. Not in his office, but in his living room, in his home, on his private island, in the middle of the Caribbean. Yes, that happened. It's funny, no matter how many times you fantasise about a moment, it's never quite how you imagine it. My trip to Necker Island was no exception.

Here was the entrepreneur who had been one of my greatest influences and inspirations, wearing his board shorts with his bare feet propped on the coffee table, as my book *Daring & Disruptive* beamed out at us from its new resting place on the bookshelf next to Nelson Mandela's *Long Walk to Freedom.* And there was me, with a massive bump on my head and a broken toe, because that morning I'd discovered a snake in my bathroom and fallen over while trying to run away with my shorts around my ankles. They say first impressions count, and my greatest inspiration wasn't going to forget me in a hurry. We shared a laugh over my misfortune, which became quite the talk of the island.

But I was hoping Richard would remember me for something else, and so rather boldly that night at dinner as I sat opposite him and surrounded by 27 other entrepreneurs, I stood up and asked him something simple. "All I ask is that you put a copy of *The Collective* in every room on Necker Island, every month," I said. "Also, that you read it yourself and, if you like it and if you have the time, think about writing some articles for us." As business pitches go, it wasn't overcomplicated, excessive or expensive. Although over the past five days

I'd grown to think of Richard as a buddy, he was also a "busy buddy", and I didn't want to ask too much. I've always believed in building relationships over time and not jamming things down people's throats. People want to do business with people they like.

And I like to think that's why, even though he famously isn't scared of saying "no" to poor investments, when I told Richard about my vision and asked for his support in growing our movement, I got a great, big "yes"! He would do it! It was an incredible, personal milestone.

This moment was a stark reminder of the power of choice, determination and vision. I've wanted to visit Necker Island for a long time, long before I had the means and contacts to get me there, when I didn't have a profile and couldn't even afford a bus ticket. And for the longest time, before I realised truly anything on this planet is possible, I thought it was completely unattainable. I have proved that theory wrong time and time again since the launch of *The Collective* and I dare say, will continue to do so. In this case, I'd somehow manifested my mission with the help of my two dear friends Billy and Fiona, who invited me along as part of a group of other entrepreneurs personally vetted by Richard.

But not only had I arrived, I'd also left my mark behind in a few ways. I don't say this to be boastful, but instead to be hopeful. If I can achieve this, then anything is possible. For all of us.

When it comes to my time on Necker Island, I could talk about the beauty of the crystal clear ocean, the pink flamingos, flying on a zip-wire from the main house to the beach, winning a sailing race past the home of Larry Page (Mr Google) or feeding the endangered species, like the Scarlet Ibis, that Richard has saved from extinction as part of his conservation program.

However, the most mind-changing aspect for me wasn't the amazing scenery or the fun activities, but seeing Richard interact with the other guests and his staff members with such empathy and compassion. Although we arrived on the island a day and a half after news broke of the Virgin Galactic crash, Richard honoured his commitments to us. He took time to chat to all of us personally, joined us for fancy-dress dinners, beach shenanigans, conga lines and impromptu dance offs (this guy knows how to party) and he generally made every single person feel special, including the Necker Island team.

I fell in love with his general managers, husband and wife team Leesa and Keny, who have worked on Necker for more than a decade and have no plans to leave anytime soon. When it comes to recruitment, Richard seeks out "ballsyness" over experience. The kitesurfing instructor Elias, who previously worked part-time in an English kitesurfing shop, joined the team after Richard put in an order for six kites and Elias slipped a note into the parcel introducing himself.

Another star employee, water-sports instructor Randy, was bored working at a neighbouring resort so one day just took a boat over to Necker, walked up to the office and asked for a job. After questioning how on earth he got onto the island, they applauded his courage and spontaneity and offered him one. That's the Branson way.

I've written a lot in this book about the importance of authenticity. Spending time around Richard really brought this home to me, as I've never met a businessman – or another human – whose morals, behaviour, characteristics, interactions, tone, look and even hobbies are so consistently aligned, with no contradictions and no apparent fakery.

Each morning I'd go walking on the beach – as best I could with aforementioned broken toe – and Richard would kitesurf by, waving. He doesn't have a desk in an office. Instead, he takes business calls from the bathtub on his deck and says his most inspiring brainwaves come while he lazes in his hammock – including the idea to launch a commercial space shuttle.

Richard is astounding without even trying, he is inspiring without being intimidating and isn't that what every leader wants to achieve? He and his wife, Joan, invited us in with open arms. I couldn't actually believe we were literally on Richard's own private island – his home.

you can't reach th

stars without an explosion

If Richard Branson is Willy Wonka, then Necker Island is his chocolate factory – a place where the impossible seems possible, where surprises lurk around every corner and he has allowed his imagination to run wild. He didn't create the culture of Necker to impress other people but to make himself happy, to build a place where he feels inspired and creative. It just so happens it has the same effect on everyone who visits. When Richard bought the island at the age of 27, he originally planned to turn it into a music studio, but then decided to keep it as a place where "extraordinary people could come, debate issues, think and have a good time". And it certainly is that.

You might not dream of going to Necker, but I hope you have your own fantasies and inspiring influences and role models. I urge you never to give up on visiting them, meeting them, matching them. Never lose sight of your vision because you think it's impractical, unmanageable or that you're not worthy.

As I looked out the window of my Necker home (the Bali Hi hut), which is Jennifer Lopez's favourite place to stay, onto a beach walked by Desmond Tutu, former US President Jimmy Carter and Princess Diana, I could have felt inadequate.

Who was I to walk in the shadows of such greatness? But I was just humbled, inspired and secretly so proud of how far I'd travelled to get here. I'd had the courage to face my role model as the truest, most authentic version of myself – bumped head, broken toe and all.

BE CAREFUL WHAT
YOU WISH FOR
(AND WHO YOU WISH TO BE)

Let's pretend that my trip to Necker Island didn't happen for a moment. I've been asked on hundreds, probably thousands of occasions, especially since the launch of *The Collective,* who my role models and mentors are and my answer has always been the same. I know that people expect me to say the usual suspects – Oprah Winfrey, Steve Jobs, Bill Gates, etc. These are all admirable people, but the reality is that I don't know them – and never expected to meet any of them until my Necker invitation. Because of this, I didn't really think of them as role models – their existence was too abstract, like a movie star playing a character, just a bunch of pixels on a screen.

I could list off a stream of multimillionaires that have become household names, but I know few of these people personally. I mostly know the marketing hype and the PR machine that surrounds them (I hope it's a true reflection but who knows really?). Have you ever heard of Sonia Sotomayor? She's a big-name judge in America, associate justice of the Supreme Court, and she put it perfectly: "Such models as appear in books or on the news, however inspiring or revered, are ultimately too remote to be real, let alone influential. But a role model in the flesh provides more than an inspiration; his or her very existence is confirmation of possibilities one may have every reason to doubt, saying, 'Yes, someone like me can do this.'"

This is why, when I'm asked about my role models, I've learned to answer the question in another way. The truth is my role models change day by day, week by week, depending on the real people who enter my life. This could be anyone that I have a face-to-face human connection with. In my line of work I'm blessed to meet a lot – and I mean a lot – of amazing people who are pursuing their greatest dreams and taking a big leap into the unknown. These are the people who are my role models; the risk takers, the thought leaders and style makers who don't have a massive corporation behind them, or a million-dollar bank account as a safety net if all fails.

Then there are the more seasoned entrepreneurs who have become good friends of mine over the years – Lorna Jane Clarkson who started life as a dental nurse and grew to be one of the greatest active wear brands, Cathie Reid and Stuart Giles who injected heart and soul into the pharmaceutical industry, leading EPIC, one of Australia's largest hospital, oncology and aged care suppliers. I could go on and on. There's Paul Schulte of the Keystone Group, who is one of the greatest thinkers and smoothest operators around, and Samantha Wills, whose jewellery brand is rapidly became a huge community and movement. When you have a chance I urge you to read up on all their career trajectories, as they really are proof that anything can be achieved (with a bucket load of determination!).

So how do you choose a role model? A recent study asked teenagers this question and found a common set of criteria: passion and an ability to inspire; a clear set of values; selflessness and acceptance of others; ability to overcome obstacles; commitment to community. On a side note – this happens to be exactly what we try to do with *The Collective*, and I'm constantly overwhelmed by the letters we get from readers who say that our magazine is their personal role model, mentoring them to follow their dreams.

Of course, a role model doesn't have to be famous. In fact, it's sometimes better if they're not. Arianna Huffington wrote a tear-jerking article about her late mother titled 'The Ultimate Fearless Role Model' in which she listed the reasons her mum was so inspiring. These ranged from extreme life experiences, such as hiding from soldiers during the Greek civil war, to everyday examples ("My mother was the ultimate non-thing person. For instance, there was the time we tried to give her a second watch for her birthday, only to have her give it to someone else two days later. 'I already have a watch,' she explained.")

A role model doesn't have to be business-based either. You can look up to someone from an emotional, professional or spiritual standing. I think that seeing someone as a role model is the antithesis of envy. It's about looking at someone, admitting you admire them but not coming at it from a place of jealousy.

Although I don't often reference pop stars (mainly because – as my staff will tell you – my finger is so far off the pulse that I never know who anyone is) but one quote from the singer Lana Del Ray stuck with me recently, "Find someone who has a life that you want and figure out how they got it. Read books, pick your role models wisely. Find out what they did and do it." I couldn't agree more!

I was lucky enough to meet Richard Branson, and so I'll place him in my role model category because he's now a real person to me (and rather excitedly, as per his quote on the front cover of this book, I am now a real person to him). But that won't stop me heralding the 'everyday heroes' of my life. While I'm all for reaching for the stars, having a role model who you actually know – in real life, not through ten degrees of separation – really does make a difference to the depths of their inspiration. When you can stand next to a role model, see they're flesh, see them breathe, and be reminded they're only human – suddenly their achievements seem even more possible to replicate. They're not hiding a superhero costume under their suit and tie. They're just like you and me. Now, that's really inspiring!

staying

humble

& grounded

On a recent holiday to Los Angeles, Jack and I got into the habit of going for an after-dinner walk most nights, generally ending in some debauched chocolate extravagance. One night we were strolling along Santa Monica Pier nearby and there were those telescopes where you put a quarter in a slot and you can look at the stars or out to sea. Jack pointed the telescopes out wistfully and said he'd love to have a go on one, but he couldn't afford it. Couldn't afford it? This from a man who, that same week, had been announced as a new entry on the Australian BRW Young Rich List? (Lists like this might focus on money and that's not what either of us are about, but they're also a measure of success and I'm super proud of Jack because it was a childhood dream of his and a huge milestone.)

But here was Jack saying he couldn't afford a quarter. And he wasn't joking. He was serious. Later that night, after I'd rumbled around unsuccessfully to find a quarter to look into space (can you believe we didn't actually have a quarter with us? Dream as yet unfulfilled…) we talked, laughed and felt intrigued by the reasons behind Jack's reaction.

When he was a child, Jack wouldn't have been able to afford to use the telescope and some things become so deeply engrained into our psyches that even when our situation is completely different, even when we've worked, achieved, chased, climbed and succeeded, we can believe we still have nothing.

Jack has the same feeling around Fruit Roll-Ups (remember those hideous snacks?) and magazines. He doesn't spend money on either – I realise now what a compliment it is that before we even met, he spent a bit of his hard-earned cash on buying mine.

I have my own quirks when it comes to this. I find it almost impossible, although I'm getting better mostly from realising how bad this is for my waistline, to leave any food at mealtimes, even if I am full. Growing up I was never allowed to leave even a pea on my plate. I hate paying for dry-cleaning, always ask for doggy bags in restaurants and never, ever eat or drink anything from hotel mini bars. Even though I now run a successful business, I still struggle to spend money on anything I couldn't afford or wasn't allowed when I was a little girl. It amazes me how people can live in abundance, yet still be trapped in a mentality of scarcity.

I didn't come from poverty, at all. I was lucky to have a comfortable childhood, a roof over my head and holidays in the sunshine (until I fled to the UK when I was 18 and refused to take any handouts from anyone). But I do know a lot of people who are doing amazing, staggering, game-changing things, who are successful but never allow themselves to feel satisfied or to sink into their abundance. I'm not just talking about an abundance of money, but the love, friendship, gratitude and warm, glowing feeling that should come with chasing your purpose. You can create the ideal life – a successful business, a close-knit family, a healthy bank balance – but if you don't allow yourself to enjoy it, all that hard work is for nothing.

This is a really interesting topic because it's a very, very fine line between self-appreciation and arrogance. There are two sides to the argument. It's about allowing yourself to pat yourself on the back, to buy yourself nice things to celebrate small victories and to share good news with your community. But you also can't let your ego get away from you and become a diva. You don't need to be a multimillionaire to find yourself in the midst of a power trip.

Since *The Collective* launched I've been in situations I never could have imagined. I've met and interviewed people like John Cleese, Martha Stewart, Ewan McGregor and Bill Clinton. I've holidayed on Richard Branson's Necker Island

with the man himself. I've been invited to attend the front-page editorial meeting at the *New York Times*. Twice. I've watched *The Collective* grow from the ground up to being distributed into more than 35 countries (and growing) and received thousands upon thousands of emails from people saying that we've helped change their lives. It would be easy to let my ego get the better of me.

I admit that some days, when a new advertising deal drops in or we've just heard the magazine has sold out at Woolworths, I can feel my metaphorical hat getting tighter as my head swells.

But the best thing about being somewhat accomplished (and having a little more available money – sometimes) is being able to give back. It buys freedom and choice. I don't want to paint the wrong picture of myself, as too butter-wouldn't-melt if you get the analogy? The truth is I am quite selfish in my selfless acts, as I get such a warm, happy feeling from giving to others.

If I'm in a bookstore or at a newsstand and I see *The Collective*, I buy a copy for anyone in the vicinity. Nothing brings me greater joy. People literally cannot believe that a) I bought them a gift when they're a stranger and b) It's the editor doing it. It costs me less than $10 per person, but the emotional payback for me is phenomenal.

WHAT REALLY MATTERS?

There is this myth that you need to be a ballbreaker to get ahead in business, that you need to bully your way to the top and, when you get there, it's then acceptable to treat everyone below you as if they're inadequate. I do not idolise *The Wolf of Wall Street* approach. I firmly believe you can be kind and successful, compassionate and profitable, ambitious and amicable.

I recently went to breakfast with a roomful of business leaders to discuss a new collaboration. Everyone around the table was from a totally different sector, and someone turned to the founder of a charity and asked him, "Do you work for a not-for-profit?" I'll never forget his answer, "Oh no, we plan to make a whole lot of profit, because without money we'll fold, and then how can we complete our purpose?" This sparked an even more interesting conversation, as the man sitting next to him – the head of a big, global company – said he couldn't agree more, but that it also worked vice versa. Just because he worked for a multinational corporation, it didn't mean they were ogres who wanted to stomp over the little guys and give nothing back. In fact, they'd started offering scholarships to smaller companies. I often talk about reciprocity – exchanging things for mutual benefit. That doesn't have to be objects or skills, it can be heartfelt greetings, support or compliments. If everyone came at life and business with a more loving, calm, open heart, rather than with fear, hate and judgement, then I believe we could accomplish so much more and make phenomenal changes.

I F**KED UP!

Okay, I didn't really f**k up. But it got your attention. And let's face it, one day I probably will do. Momentously! I'm not perfect, a genius or invincible and I'm actually amazed that I've managed to launch a magazine with zero experience and haven't yet made a huge blooper. Clearly the universe is smiling on me.

I hope it doesn't happen but if, in years down the track, I make a financial mistake, discover a flaw in my business plan or accidentally offend someone with my decisions, I will ask for one thing: compassion. Of every topic I've touched on in this book, this is probably the most important. So grab a highlighter pen and scribble all over this bit!

The problem with building a platform, with creating a personal profile as I've done to give *The Collective*'s community a centre point, is that you leave yourself vulnerable and your actions are under constant scrutiny. They say it takes 20 years to build a profile, and 20 minutes to tear it down. Even if you're not an entrepreneur you'll recognise that feeling.

We live in a culture where people are constantly comparing, competing and judging. Even reality TV shows often promote arguments and the entire format is set up to encourage feuding. Our culture has normalised this unloving, un-nurturing, angry society.

It doesn't feel very nice does it? But why do we accept that society has to be that way? We can be agents for change – even if it's just our own reactions, mindsets and opinions. If an entrepreneur, a mother, a friend makes an innocent mistake, does that mean everything else they've achieved, the joy they've manifested, the lives they've changed, no longer count for anything?

Let's stop tearing each other down and disguising it as ambition. Let's stop living isolated, self-involved lives and saying it's "just the modern way of living". My entire purpose when creating *The Collective* was to spread stories of love, hope and inspiration. They said good never sells, but we've proved otherwise. If you are doing something great in the world and you believe in yourself, then use it to connect with people, to start a conversation. And if someone else says they have an idea, then listen – you never know what they might tell you. I believe people are genuinely good under all the bullsh*t and masks that we sometimes wear. And if you empower them, connect with them, make them feel a part of something important to you and what you are growing – if you give them a reason to help you – then nine times out of 10 they will.

Expect nothing.
Appreciate

everything.

a surpris

e ending

only intended to write 10 chapters in this book, but then I got the surprise ending of my life. And I have my fiancé – yes, I said fiancé – to thank for it. What better way to finish a book called *Life & Love* than with a proposal on the day of the cover shoot? I hinted earlier on that our photo shoot had been unforgettable –

I wasn't exaggerating.

I did wonder why, at the very end of the day, the photographer, Scott, suggested we go back to the little, white bridge where we'd already shot a ton of photos – a nostalgic spot where I used to play and feed the ducks with my grandmother when I was little – some of my most beautiful memories.

I had hardly eaten anything all day and all I could think about was going home, getting in my trackies, watching a movie and eating a big bag of chips on the couch (even the most healthy of us fall off the wagon sometimes). As we approached our final location and I saw a guy standing on the bridge with his back to us, I wondered if he'd mind moving to let us take some pics. I got closer and I realised it was Jack – who had told me he was busy catching up with the boys when I had asked him to come along and have a pic with me for the love chapter. And as I got even closer, there were big bunches of flowers tied to the bridge. I was dizzy. Nothing was making sense. You know when you see someone completely out of context and your brain just doesn't compute? Why was the bridge covered in flowers? What was going on?

It was all such a blur that I only know what Jack said because he repeated it to

me later, "I love you so much. It doesn't matter if we're billionares living between Paris, Rome and New York City or as a housewife and househusband living in Bangalow, all that matters is that we do it together because that's what makes us happy." I said a big fat, "Yes, yes, yes!" amidst all the incredible, hazy, delirium.

The most amazing aspect of this story is that I didn't suspect it was going to happen – despite the fact that in the few weeks leading up to it, I'd been on high alert waiting for a proposal. My good friend Cathie described me as Defcon 4 – Google the reference and you'll understand how vigilant I was! I was 100 per cent sure it would happen during our holiday on Necker Island. I was 100 per cent sure I wanted it to. In my mind it was the perfect setting. I may have also dropped just a few hints (uhum!) because on our last night in Necker, as we lay in bed after midnight, Jack suddenly told me, "Get up, it's going to happen now."

He led me down to the beach, both of us barefoot, both of us butt naked (don't try this at home!) and because he didn't have a ring, he asked me to take off a ring my aunty gave me for my 21st birthday and hand it to him. But then (and you won't believe this) a big wave crashed onto the sand where we were standing and my ring was washed out of his hand and lost into the water. Jack was mortified and thought I'd be cranky, but how could I be? For one, it was an accident. In a funny way, I love that I lost it on Necker, because now it means a piece of me will always be there, my own personal shipwreck. But more importantly, it was symbolic of the personal metamorphosis occuring, another chance for new beginnings. I saw it as a clear message from the universe – stop rushing, stop micromanaging, stop 'rowing the boat' as I spoke about in the love chapter. Everything in that moment was just as it should be. It was perfect.

In *Daring & Disruptive* I wrote a lot about detachment from outcomes and surrendering to the natural order in which events unfold, and this was a perfect example – and a test for me – to practise what I preach. I thought a proposal on Necker would be perfect, but what Jack came up with was even better: a three-stage proposal that started in the park, followed by an amazing candlelit picnic on

Camp Cove beach in Sydney with a gourmet feast of every food group imaginable, then I returned home to find he'd filled our bedroom and bathroom with flowers – 20+ huge bouquets and hundreds of candles! It was so romantic – down to the sparkling apple juice he'd bought instead of champagne. This is a man who could afford to propose at the fanciest restaurant but knows that I'm at my happiest barefoot on the sand, and that no matter how successful I am, that will never change. We celebrated our engagement a few evenings later by inviting our friends to have fish and chips with us on the beach. I couldn't think of a better way.

I want to finish up by sharing one more piece of proof that your own actions can have a butterfly effect; that creating a small pocket of happiness, joy and love can affect more people than you ever imagined. The day after our engagement, Jack and I went out with my dad for Yum Cha.

We were standing in the queue, showing my dad the engagement photos on my iPad, and suddenly the woman behind us in line says, "Excuse me, but did you get engaged in Centennial Park yesterday?"

She then pulled out her iPhone and showed us a photo she'd taken – a bridge covered in flowers and a paper sign that read: "Please don't touch. Proposal taking place at 5pm". She must have walked past the spot half an hour before I got there. It had made her well up with love and so, in turn, she decided to post it on Instagram and share the joy. Jack's act of love didn't only make me the happiest girl on the planet, but had a far greater reach, as the story travelled far, far beyond the people we know.

Within an hour of announcing our engagement on Instagram, the photo had over 1200 likes and hundreds of comments such as, "Romance isn't dead. This gives me hope." I can tell you it's far from dead and I've experienced love and connectedness with Jack that is beyond the realms of what I've ever imagined possible. While I'm so humbled by the people who look at my life – my business, my relationship, my happiness – and think that we're aspirational, I hope they also read this book and see the journey it took me to get here, and why the hard work, the self-exploration, the courage, the risks, the leaps and the terrifying new beginnings are all so worth it. Imagine if I'd stopped moving, pursuing, pushing myself in my twenties or thirties, and everything I would have missed out on now.

I hope this book has helped you to realise you can be anything, and everything, all at once. You can be strong and vulnerable, you can be driven and nurturing, you can be passionate and peaceful, you have the capacity to live and love – large! I started this book by saying I'm deliriously happy and I'm finishing the book even happier. I didn't think that was possible when I wrote chapter one, but it turns out every story can have an unexpected twist. Where will yours take you?

love

And I'd choose you;
in a hundred lifetimes,
in a hundred worlds,
in any version of reality,

I'd find you and
I'd choose you.

—the Chaos of Stars

ABOUT THE AUTHOR

Lisa Messenger is the vibrant, game-changing CEO and creative director of The Messenger Group, as well as founder and editor-in-chief of *The Collective* magazine – an entrepreneurial and lifestyle magazine distributed into more than 35 countries with a mandate to disrupt, challenge and inspire. In addition, she has worked globally in events, sponsorship, marketing, PR and publishing.

Lisa has authored and co-authored over a dozen books and The Messenger Group has custom published more than 400 books for companies and individuals. Lisa is a regular commentator on business, entrepreneurialism and property and has sat on a number of boards including the Australian Businesswomen's Network and Publishers Australia.

She's trekked across India raising money for charity, ridden camels in the Sahara for fun and has laughed her way through communal showers in the Costa Rican jungle in the name of personal development.

Her passion is to challenge individuals and corporations to change the way they think, take them out of their comfort zone and prove that there is more than one way to do anything. She encourages entrepreneurial spirit, creativity and innovation and always lives life to the absolute max. Most mornings she wakes up and pinches herself as to how incredible her life is, but Lisa is also acutely aware and honest about the bumps and tumbles along the way. In between being a serial entrepreneur and avid traveller, she spends most of her time in Sydney with her partner Jack and their beautiful dog, Benny.

SPEAKING OPPORTUNITIES

Lisa is available for speaking opportunities. Her key message is "anything's possible".

Her presentation is highly engaging, active, motivational and really gets people wanting to jump out of their seats and take on the world!

Lisa uses a lot of tools, anecdotes, stories, how-to's and self-deprecating humour to take her audience on the journey.

Some of Lisa's favourite topics to speak on are:
- strategic partnerships,
- building a personal and business brand,
- cultivating your self-belief,
- challenging your personal limits and overall thinking,
- how to disrupt in business and within a corporate,
- trusting your gut instinct, and;
- finding passion and purpose in everything that you do.

For more information, bookings and bulk book sales enquiries email info@themessengergroup.com.au or phone +61 2 9699 7216

RENEGADE COLLECTIVE

The Collective is a monthly 176-page entrepreneurial and lifestyle magazine that brings together entrepreneurial and creative minds from across the globe and is distributed in more than 35 countries. It's a community that appeals to game changers, rule breakers, thought leaders and style makers with a common appetite for challenging the status quo.

Through personal stories, in-depth interviews, investigative features and practical tips, *The Collective* aims to inspire and inform. Whether you are looking for a new idea to tackle, business advice from industry professionals or a friendly dose of encouragement, *The Collective* is your guide to making an impact in this world.

COLLECTIVE HUB

More than just a print magazine, the Collective Hub global community is engaged across a number of platforms that echo the same philosophies found within our pages. We are reaching out to our readers wherever they are in the world through events, collaborations, strategic partnerships, our ambassador program and ultimately continuing the conversation through our online hubs.

WEBSITE *collectivehub.com*
FACEBOOK *facebook.com/collectivehub*
INSTAGRAM *@lisamessenger #lifeandlove*
@collectivehub #collectivehub
TWITTER *@lisamessenger #lifeandlove*
@collectivehub #collectivehub

BESPOKE CONTENT CREATION

WHAT YOU MAY NOT KNOW ABOUT US:

Before the launch of *The Collective* magazine, The Messenger Group was a custom publishing, integrated marketing and branding agency first and foremost. Since 2001, we have been crafting thoughtfully designed and creative content for a multitude of leading brands, companies and individuals across both print and digital mediums.

WHAT WE CAN DO FOR YOU:

Combining our expertise in branding, public relations, content creation, community management and marketing, we are specialists in delivering the stories our clients want to tell. By tapping into the power of captivating content, we can assist in encouraging a two-way conversation between company and consumer.

HOW WE CAN HELP:

By designing and creating content for a variety of:

- Print media (books, journals, diaries, magazines)
- Digital media
- Commerce-enabled websites

We can be your copywriter, videographer and social media strategist or we can tailor bespoke content packages to your specific requirements.

For general enquiries please email info@themessengergroup.com.au
For more information see collectivehub.com

ACKNOWLEDGEMENTS

Massive thanks to my incredible team who love and support me every single day to be the best version of myself. Big shout out to the core team – Claire, Mel, Jade, Tash, Edie, Tara, Kayla, Phoebe, Asha, Britt, Jodie, Kate and Amy.

Big shout out to Amy and Mel for helping me to structure my thoughts and pull out the best in me. To Jade and Edie for putting my vision perfectly on the page. And to Claire and Jodes for securing the most extraordinary distribution and working with me to really make these babies move and find a big place in this world. You are all incredible and helped make this book happen at an extraordinary and alarming pace – we certainly don't do things by halves and I love having you all by my side on this crazy, fast-paced, high-growth journey.

Our extended team of 37+ distributors and roughly 70 writers around the globe. A special mention goes out to Jodie Frazer, Shayne McNally, Trevor West, Scott Snodgrass, Janet Judge, Dennis Jones, Victoria Harper, Hunter Drinan and Warren Broom.

Thanks to my gorgeous family – Mum, Dad, Kate, Dennis, Margot, Mick and Gracie.

And to my amazing partner Jack for loving and supporting me through this journey every single day. You are without a doubt the most incredible human I have ever met.

Thank you to our incredible readers, who cheer us on and support and inspire me every single day. Thanks to you, the movement is growing and we are inspiring positive change in this world. xx

HAVEN'T READ THE PREQUEL YET? DON'T MISS *DARING & DISRUPTIVE: UNLEASHING THE ENTREPRENEUR*

Daring & Disruptive is an insightful and soulful account of the entrepreneur's roller-coaster ride for those who want to succeed almost as much as they want to breath… who want to make the impossible possible and the ordinary extraordinary.

Lisa Messenger blends her personal stories with the important business lessons she has learned along the way, from why money is not the only currency to how to fail well.

Lisa gives readers a valuable insight into her world, whether you're a budding entrepreneur, seasoned game changer or a corporate ladder-climber dreaming of creating your own gig or making positive change from the inside. This book will help you dig deep, stay on purpose, back yourself, be true to your ideas, and ensure that if you're thrown to the wolves, you'll have the strength to come out leading the pack. Your life is your message to the world. So embrace the journey and live it out loud.

"Business anarchy for fun and profit – not for the short of breath, weak of spine or faint of heart. Put on clean underwear and turn to page one."
BRADLEY TREVOR GREIVE, AM,
NEW YORK TIMES BEST-SELLING AUTHOR

DARING & DISRUPTIVE: THE PLAYBOOK

Do you want to unleash your inner entrepreneur? With prompts, exercises and tons of space to brainstorm your creative process, the *Daring & Disruptive Playbook* (so called, because hopefully it won't feel like work) will guide you through the process of finding your 'why', identifying your purpose and helping you break free of traditional thinking around what a career should look like. Disclaimer: this isn't like any other business planning template you've ever read. Neither will it spoonfeed you the answers. But, by the final page, you'll have created a manifesto of your dream workday, identified the corner of the world you want to change and how you're going to do it.

LIFE & LOVE: THE PLAYBOOK

Do you want to be ambitious but loving, successful but compassionate, driven but feminine – and most of all, happy?

This playbook is designed to be read in tandem with *Life & Love*. With exercises, tasks, prompts and plenty of room to unleash your creativity, this playbook is a springboard to help you look within, identify the areas of your life that you love, and explore ways to make constructive changes to ensure you live the life you want.

Wondering how can you find your purpose, while still making time for your friends, family, health, community and the simple pleasures that ground you? There are enough hours in the week for everything that matters (with a few secret strategies and savvy prioritising)! Whether you're an entrepreneur, a creative, a parent, a friend, or all of the above, this playbook is a canvas to help you to design a life you love.

GET YOUR COPY OR FOR MORE INFORMATION

COLLECTIVEHUB.COM

*Thanks for reading
& sharing your thoughts
with the world.
Humbled & grateful.
x Lisa*

WHAT READERS ARE SAYING ABOUT *DARING & DISRUPTIVE...*
(SOCIAL MEDIA, EMAIL AND BOOK REVIEWS)

Nelson Mandela. Maya Angelou. Princess Diana. Jim Stynes. Samantha Wills. Each one has inspired both my personal and professional journey beyond measures. Today, I'm adding Lisa Messenger to that list. I'm not sure I even have the words to do this book justice. It's everything. It speaks to my core and makes my heart burst with gratitude. It's ignited the fire within my soul that was all but extinguished over the last few years and it's given me fuel to chase my dreams once again. Thank you for being you, thank you for words that resonate so easily with my heart and core and thank you for giving me back the little girl who had the biggest dreams but was trampled by life.

JUANITA POWELL

*Amaze-balls. Life altering!
I'm shattered. Have just read this book in one sitting. No bookmark required. I ran out of highlighter pens half way through. As an entrepreneur/artist/content creator/ designer with a squillion ginormous ideas every five seconds, my heart is singing louder than ever since reading Lisa's journey. If it can be IMAGINED... it can be CREATED. Never let anyone tell you it can't be done.
So much juicy soul food in this book. Thank you!*

MEL THE CREATIVE, BYRON BAY

I'm glad it came with a free cardboard bookmark as it has now been ripped to pieces to mark all my favourite pages. Amongst all the lessons and inspiration, my fav is when you wrote about culture and making sure each professional relationship cultivated is mutually beneficial, as I strongly believe "the people make the place".

JACINTA MANGAN

Thoroughly enjoyed this book, and managed to fit in a chapter even when I was snowed under with business and "didn't really have time". You really do have the same number of hours in your day as Richard Branson.

JANNA, PERTH

Reading your book on the plane, I was in tears of recognition and inspiration. I cried, I laughed, I felt deeply inspired. I love how you mix sharing your gifts with the world together with making a difference, purpose, creativity, listening to yourself, caring deeply for others, growing as a human being, and the beauty of words and pictures.

MARION ROSE

It's really encouraging to hear about your journey and the hurdles and set-backs you refer to, it reminded me of all that I have experienced, felt and learnt. The past two years have been crazy for me - everything in my world has been shaken. Some much of what you said today was uncannily serendipitous and stupidly obvious (I am referring to myself reflecting on the obvious) but most importantly, it was that little boost, that reminder to keep going. To dust my knees off, pick myself and get back out there.

JACLYN

You're disrupting my nap time @lisamessenger. I love a good afternoon nap while the kido winds down after school but I cannot put this book down! Any free moment is another few pages of inspiration! #igetgoosebumps #icry #daringanddisruptive.

ELLE ROBERTS

I've been worried that motherhood might slow me down from pursuing the incessant entrepreneurial ideas that come to me and go no further than my notebook. After 30 minutes of rocking bub in the pram to sleep and 40 pages into @lisamessenger's new book however, my self-belief is telling (yelling/roaring) me otherwise. Thank you to Lisa for being such a strong force of encouragement and source of inspiration. #pumped #believer.

MICHELLE ROLDAN BOYD

Perfect Saturday night in. Reading #daringanddisruptive by @lisamessenger editor of collectivehub #greatread. A must for all entrepreneurs.

FLEUR WOOD

Inspirational and uplifting, thought-provoking, game changing words in my hands. This book speaks volumes to me - thank you @lisamessenger for words of wisdom, down-to-earth no bullsh*t content. It's just what I needed to read. Thank YOU.

JESS VISCARDE

I am currently laying in the sun in a #blissful state of #brainexplosion having #inspirationoverload, due to reading @lisamessenger's new book #daringanddisruptive. This is the best so called lazy afternoon, spent ever! If you have been waiting for "that inspirational sign" to #start or "follow your dreams" this book, definitely is it! Just brilliant.

GEORGIA RHODES

Lisa's humility, grace and positive spirit instil a deep aspiration in my mind and soul to chase my dreams, my desires, my passions. She's taught me to take on risks, fail fast, fail often… it will be okay - it all happens for a reason and I will be all the better because of it. She's my role model, mentor, fairy godmother (emoji) and her amazing mind continually astounds me.

RACHEL KARETA

Oh Miss Messenger! This book makes me feel reconnected to that fire in my belly. That zest and passion to create. The desire to reinvent beyond imagination. Dig deep. Believe. Just believe! Times are changing and I am grateful for this fine lady to be telling us to be daring and disruptive. Devouring each page.

SALLY-ANNE BLANSHARD

Daring & Disruptive *by Lisa Messenger… I've read a few motivational books but this one is by far the best. It has empowered me to just START!*

KAT CHARLY

I cried reading the intro! Touched me. Love your honesty and authenticity.

PAIGE HIGHAM